COME DOWN ZACCHAEUS

Other books by Thomas H. Green, S.J.
    OPENING TO GOD
    WHEN THE WELL RUNS DRY
    DARKNESS IN THE MARKETPLACE
    WEEDS AMONG THE WHEAT
    A VACATION WITH THE LORD

COME DOWN ZACCHAEUS

Spirituality & The Laity

Thomas H. Green, s.j.

AVE MARIA PRESS
Notre Dame, IN 46556

Acknowledgments

The scripture quotations contained in Part One are from the Revised Standard Version Common Bible, copyright 1973 by the Division of Christian Education of the National Council of the Churches of Christ in the USA, and are used by permission.

The scripture texts used in Part Two are from THE JERUSALEM BIBLE, copyright © 1966 by Darton, Longman & Todd, Ltd. and Doubleday & Company, Inc. Used by permission of the publisher.

Excerpts from the Documents of Vatican II, Walter M. Abbott, S.J. and Joseph Gallagher, eds., reprinted with permission of America Press, Inc., 106 West 56th Street, New York, NY 10019. © 1966. All rights reserved.

Lines from "Little Gidding" from FOUR QUARTETS by T.S. Eliot, copyright 1936 by Harcourt Brace Jovanovich, Inc.; copyright © 1963, 1964 by T.S. Eliot. Reprinted by permission of the publisher.

Imprimi potest
Rev. Bienvenido F. Nebres, S.J.
Provincial, Philippines Province
June 1, 1987

Nihil obstat
Msgr. Josefino S. Ramirez
Vicar General and Censor

Imprimatur
Jaime Cardinal L. Sin
Archbishop of Manila
April 13, 1987

© 1988 by Ave Maria Press, Notre Dame, Indiana 46556

International Standard Book Number: 0-87793-373-1

Library of Congress Catalog Card Number: 87-72256

Cover design: Elizabeth J. French

Printed and bound in the United States of America.

♨ Contents

♨ *Introduction*

The Age of the Laity

Going Home Again After Vatican II

For Roman Catholics, the most significant religious event of the past 50 years has been the Second Vatican Council, convoked by Pope John XXIII in 1962, continued by his successor, Pope Paul VI, and concluded in 1965. It was an attempt to bring the church into living dialogue with the modern world, to make the gospel relevant to the men and women of our own time.

The scope of the council was vast. In the 16 documents approved by the 2,000 bishops in the council and promulgated by Pope Paul VI, almost every area of modern life was explored in the light of faith: war and peace, birth control, social justice, the development of nations and international relations, the liturgy of the Mass and the sacraments, spirituality, ecumenism and interfaith relations, even the role of the United Nations.

One of the experts it called upon for advice was John Courtney Murray, S.J., who played a principal role in formulating the breakthrough decree on religious liberty. Father Murray was one of my professors at that time at Woodstock College in Maryland. I recall vividly his return from one of the sessions. Some of us asked him what the council was really all about, what its real meaning for us was. He replied that no one really knew the answer to that except the Holy Spirit. Not even the bishops who voted on the decrees, he said, really knew what the council meant in God's design. It would take us 50 years to see clearly what the Spirit was doing.

December 1985 was the 20th anniversary of the conclusion of the Second Vatican Council. We are less than halfway through Father Murray's 50 years, and his words come often to my mind. It seems clear to me today how right he was: We have only begun to digest its implications for Catholic and Christian life. For some people it changed too much, for others, too little. But one thing seems clear: The church of the postconciliar age can never return to the days before 1963. The vernacular liturgy, the new thrust for social justice even among and by formerly "sacristy (or convent) bound" sisters and priests, the basic Christian communities, parish councils, diocesan senates of priests, national episcopal conferences, and the focus on the Eucharist as medicine and strength for the sick more than a reward for the already holy are just some of the signs that we have indeed entered a new age. To borrow Thomas Wolfe's fascinating book title, it seems clear that, for better or worse, we "can't go home again."

Not everyone is happy about this fact. For some, the "good old days" are greatly lamented. And we all must admit that something has been lost—a certain security or stability, perhaps, in knowing that the church at least remained unchanged in the midst of rapid and unsettling development in other areas of our life. When two people marry, they inevitably experience loss as well as gain. No matter how much they love one another, they will know aching moments of realization that they can no longer go home again to Mama and Papa.

To continue the analogy, the newly married will be able to break with the past only if they understand and appreciate what they are building, only if they love one another enough to desire to risk the unknown hand-in-hand. Similarly every Catholic (or even every Christian, since virtually all the Christian churches have experienced ferment and rapid change in the past 20 or 30 years)—if he or she is to risk encountering the Lord in this new age—must explore the changed world into which the Holy Spirit, in Vatican II, has led us.

I think we can *begin* to answer the question we seminarians posed to Father Murray long ago: What really is the meaning of the council for Catholic (and Christian) life in the late 20th century? We in the Catholic church, I believe, are moving into what we can rightly call "the age of the laity." In the chapters to follow I would like to explore this personal insight with you to stimulate your own thinking about what it means to you to be Christian and Catholic today.

The Call of Zacchaeus

I chose to call the book *Come Down, Zacchaeus*, since I feel the Zacchaeus story is a paradigm for the emerging age of the laity. Only Luke, with his concern for the social dimension of the Good News of Jesus, tells us the story of Zacchaeus of Jericho (Lk 19:1-10).

In Luke's gospel, the most literary and polished of the four, Jesus makes but a single journey to Jerusalem during his public ministry. Luke uses the single journey as a symbol of Jesus' whole mission and vocation. The journey is presented from the outset as a dramatic movement toward Jesus' being "taken up," the paschal mystery of his passion, resurrection and ascension which awaits him in the city of David.

The dramatic tension increases throughout the chapters, leading in chapter 19 to the account of Jesus' arrival in the city of his destiny. Strikingly, his encounter with Zacchaeus in Jericho is the final incident on the journey itself. "He entered Jericho and was passing through. And there was a man named Zacchaeus; he was a chief tax collector, and rich" (Lk 19:1-2).

The tax collectors were a despised class in Jesus' time—despised because they enriched themselves by

working for the colonial government of Rome and thus
betraying their own people and nation.

Such people as prostitutes and tax collectors, public
sinners, play an especially prominent role in the gospel of
Luke. They represent the outcasts to whom the Good
News of Jesus seems to be especially directed. He came
not for the well but for the sick; and he himself even
came to be known as "a glutton and a drunkard, a friend
of tax collectors and sinners"(Lk 7:34). While he did not
love their vices but always called them to conversion,
Jesus did love *them*—perhaps because their very situation
as public outcasts left them stripped naked of pretence
and hypocrisy. They could be genuine in a way that the
"pillars of the church" often could not. Thus it was that
Zacchaeus, having very little reputation to defend, could
afford to make a fool of himself in his desire to see Jesus:
"And he sought to see who Jesus was, but could not, on
account of the crowd, because he was small of stature. So
he ran on ahead and climbed up into a sycamore tree to
see him, for he was to pass that way"(Lk 19:3-4).

A beautiful passage in the gospel of John (1:35-51)
can help us understand the call of Zacchaeus. He re-
counts here the call of the first five disciples of Jesus.
And, as is characteristic of John, he gives us not so much
a comprehensive account of the facts (we know from the
other evangelists that there were really 12 called to be
apostles) but a "theology" of vocation. In each case—first
Andrew and John himself, then Peter, Philip and finally,
Nathanael—God always makes the first move, he draws
us to himself, either directly (as in the case of Philip) or
through a human instrument like John the Baptist.

In John's gospel, Jesus tells us: "No one can come to
me unless the Father who sent me draws him"(Jn 6:44).
God always makes the first move; he draws us to himself.
But God's drawing never forces us to respond. The Lord
always leaves us free to respond to his gracious initiative.

This was true of Andrew and John, who freely followed Jesus and asked him, "Rabbi, where do you live?" (1:38). And, John is telling us, it is true of every call to faith and discipleship.

We see this pattern in the story of Zacchaeus. The Lord put into this tax collector's heart a desire to see and to hear Jesus. Zacchaeus was free to respond to this desire, and respond he did, even to the extent of forgetting his dignity and pride by climbing up into the sycamore tree. This one "foolish" act, a response to the gracious drawing of God, was to transform Zacchaeus' whole life. "And when Jesus came to the place, he looked up and said to him, 'Zacchaeus, make haste and come down; for I must stay at your house today.' So he did make haste and came down, and received him joyfully. And when they saw it they all murmured, 'He has gone in to be the guest of a man who is a sinner' " (Lk 19:5-7).

There is a third aspect to John's theology of vocation: Not only does God always make the first move, and leave us free to respond to his gracious initiative, but he also deals with each of us in a uniquely personal way. He changes the name of the impetuous and impressionable Peter; he simply calls the unimaginative Philip without any dramatic flourishes; and he discusses scriptural exegesis with Nathanael, the good Pharisee. The Lord takes his followers where he finds them, and deals with them according to their personalities, gifts and states in life.

Similarly, his call to each of us is personal and unique. Peter, John, Andrew and the other apostles were called to leave everything to follow Jesus. Apparently, though, Zacchaeus never heard their call. For this reason I chose him as the patron of our reflections on lay spirituality. He was called to discipleship and to holiness while remaining in the world of his ordinary life. That seems clear from his toast to Jesus at his home, "And Zacchaeus

stood and said to the Lord, 'Behold, Lord, the half of my
goods I give to the poor; and if I have defrauded any one
of anything, I restore it fourfold.' And Jesus said to him,
'Today salvation has come to this house, since this man
also is a son of Abraham. For the Son of man came to
seek and to save the lost' "(Lk 19:8-10).

Zacchaeus *did* have to make sacrifices, to change his
way of life, if he was to become a true disciple of Jesus.
He had to share his goods with the poor and make
restitution to those whom he had defrauded. Conversion
is always costly, since it necessarily involves breaking with
our sinful and selfish attachments. But it does not necessarily involve entering a convent or a seminary, or renouncing marriage and possessions. Leaving everything
for the gospel is not the only way, the usual way, nor even
necessarily the better way. In the real world, the better
way is that to which God is calling *me*. Each person must
discover that unique call, and then live it with full generosity.

The story of Zacchaeus has always been a favorite of
the church, as it is a favorite of mine. When I began to
think about writing on lay spirituality, Zacchaeus came
immediately to mind. I see a symbolic meaning in the
details of his call. He thought he could only see Jesus if
he climbed the sycamore tree. But when the Lord passed
by, he called him down: "Zacchaeus, make haste and
come down; for I must stay at your house today." Zacchaeus did not have to climb the tree of celibacy or religious life in order to see Jesus. He could encounter him
right on the ground of his ordinary life. That, in fact, is
where Jesus desired to encounter him, not in the celibate
tree, but right in his own home where he lived his lay life.

This realization about Zacchaeus led me to reflect
that probably most of those called by Jesus during his
ministry shared the vocation of the little man in the tree. I
was delighted when Luke's gospel alone yielded no less

than 16 other accounts of people who shared the call of Zacchaeus. I think it is worth listing them, just to impress upon our hearts and minds the reality and importance of the lay vocation in the gospel. My list begins with Simon's mother-in-law (4:38-39); then the paralytic who "went home" (5:17-26); the centurion (7:1-10); the widow of Nain (7:11-17); the woman who was a sinner and Simon (7:36-50); the Gerasene demoniac who "went off home" (8:26-39); the woman with the hemorrhage, and Jairus and his daughter (8:40-56); the epileptic demoniac and his father (9:37-43); Martha and Mary (10:38-42); the crippled woman on the sabbath (13:10-17); the grateful Samaritan leper (17:11-19); the rich aristocrat or "young man"—a special case, since he was called to leave everything but declined the call (18:18-27); the Jericho blind man (18:35-43); the widow with her mite (21:1-4); the good thief on Calvary (23:39-43); and, finally, the women at the Easter Tomb (24:1-11).

The very length of the list is impressive. It makes clear that the lay vocation, as we would call it today, was a very important part of the kingdom of God which Jesus proclaimed and established. It also makes clear that the call of Zacchaeus is not without cost. All who encountered Jesus found their lives radically transformed. And yet, paradoxically, they did not have to leave home (their daily concerns and responsibilities) in order to live with him. It was he who transformed their home—and not they who abandoned it!

The Church as a Pyramid

Why speak of the call of Zacchaeus as a new vision of the church *after* Vatican II? Since his story is part of the New Testament revelation, has not the lay vocation always been recognized as a legitimate and valuable way of following Christ? Yes and no. There have always been lay saints, like Martha and Thomas More and King Louis IX of France. But the common tendency has been to think of

lay Catholics as somehow second-class Christians. To
follow Jesus fully and wholeheartedly has usually been
taken to mean living a celibate religious or priestly life.

Even scripture could be cited in defense of this view.
Paul says that "he who marries his betrothed does well;
and he who refrains from marriage will do even better" (1
Cor 7:38). Though it is perhaps misguided if we consider
closely the concrete historical context of Paul's saying, the
traditional tendency has been to take Paul's words as
literal and universal—celibacy is always and for everyone a
"higher" form of discipleship.

In the Philippines, we bring eggs to the Poor Clare
nuns when we want good weather. The practice could be
expressive of a beautiful, simple trust in the Lord. But it
could also be done because we believe that they are closer
to God, more influential with him, because of their
cloistered, consecrated lives. Similarly, when we accord
the clergy places of honor in our gatherings and the best
food, we may reflect a distorted vision of the gospel
teaching. The desire to honor Christ in his representatives
is surely laudable; but we may not be acting according to
the mind of Jesus himself, who washed his disciples' feet
and commanded them to do as he had done.

We might say that our image or model of the church
has been that of a pyramid, with the pope at the pinnacle
and the laity at the base. Between the two extremes we
find, in descending order, the bishops, the clergy and the
members of religious orders. The more one ascends the
pyramid, the closer to God he or she is—holier, *more*
Christian. This has led to practices and attitudes that
overvalue clergy and religious and undervalue laypeople.
Thus when the mother of a priest dies, we are likely to
hear a funeral homily in which she is praised and hon-
ored as the mother of a priest (or sister), without any
reference to her other children who were just "ordinary"
Christians. Her priest-son is her crowning glory because

he was higher on the pyramid of holiness than the rest of her children.

What is wrong, you might ask, with this pyramid-model of the church and the practices it has engendered? In attempting to answer that question, in the next section I will suggest that the Second Vatican Council proposed a significantly different model to Catholics today. We might say that the council *inverted* the pyramid and in so doing opened up a whole new (or renewed) vision of what it means to be a disciple of Jesus Christ. It is because of this that I believe we can speak of this post-Vatican II age as the "age of the laity" in the church. But a pyramid is an unusually stable geometrical form. It is difficult to turn it upside down and balance it on its tip. Even when we understand and accept the church's teaching, we may still bring eggs to the Poor Clares—just to be safe!

Inverting the Pyramid

I proposed above that the core meaning of the council is its "new" vision of the church and of the meaning of Christian discipleship. In one sense, the vision is not new: It is that of Jesus and of the scriptural revelation, as all authentic Catholic doctrine must be. But it is new relative to the pyramidal model of Christian life and holiness which has dominated our thinking for several centuries now. That is, we have tended to think of holiness in a hierarchical way: The higher one rose on the pyramid, with the laity at the base and the various religious and clergy in ascending steps up to the pope at the top, the closer one came to God. Concretely, to be a celibate priest or religious was seen as a more perfect way of following Christ than the married state. To be married was, in some perhaps vague way, to be a second-class Christian or Catholic.

Vatican II turned this pyramid upside down, so that the base became the top. In searching for an image to describe the church today, the bishops in the council considered several, including the Mystical Body of Christ made central by Pope Pius XII in the decades before the council. The body metaphor, derived from St. Paul, had the great advantage of stressing the mutual interdependence of all the members of the church. No part is more important than any other, since each has its own proper and essential role to play in the healthy functioning of the whole body.

Indeed, the documents of Vatican II use the mystical body metaphor more than 20 times. It comes very close to the vision of the church on which the council wished to ground its dialogue with the contemporary world. I think we could say, though, that another image is even more central to the council's vision: the "People of God," a societal rather than a biological metaphor. The image has strong biblical roots, since Israel was, above all, the people of Yahweh—a people chosen from all the nations of the earth to be uniquely his own (Dt 14:2).

From this perspective, we come before the Lord as a community. It scarcely makes sense to say that some member or class is more Catholic, holier, more precious to Yahweh than any other. Before we are eyes or ears or toes, we are *one* as his body. Our being lay or religious or clergy, pope or bishop or father of a family, is a function within our identity as a community. This is why I suggested that the council "inverted" the pyramid, placing the people of God, the whole community, at the top. Then in *descending* order we have the religious, the clergy, the bishops, and finally, at the bottom, the pope. They, of course, are all part of the community, the people of God. In this sense the inverted pyramid image may not be entirely satisfactory, but it does bring out one important fact: No role in the church produces superior, more perfect Christians—closer to Christ and God—than the "ordinary" Christian. Rather, bishops, clergy, religious and lay people each have particular roles of service to play within the community according to their calls.

To take myself as an example, my being a priest is not a claim to a fuller Christianity than my married brother and sister, but a call to serve the people of God in a particular way. Beautiful as my priestly role is, it is not the defining reality of my life. What defines my Christianity is my being part of the people consecrated to God in Christ Jesus. I share this defining identity equally with every member of the church—with each of you who belongs to Christ as I do.

I suggested earlier that this conciliar vision of the church as the people of God is not really new. It is the vision of Jesus in the gospels, in John 15, for example. But we have not been accustomed to think of ourselves in this way, nor has it been easy for most of us to grasp the implications of its reaffirmation by the council. Once we have "inverted the pyramid" in our own thinking, the purpose of Part One of this book, we will be able in Part Two to explore the implications of this inversion for our life of faith and service. That inversion, I believe, was the real work of the Holy Spirit in Vatican II.

Confronting Three Devil's Myths

If we ask why the age of the laity has been so slow in dawning in the church, we could say—as we will in Part Two below—that the answer is to be found by reviewing the history of the evolution of Christian spirituality. But if we look deeper and ask why our history is as it is, we have to acknowledge that the devil has been at work. That he is very much involved in our history, as he was in the life of Jesus himself, is basic to the whole biblical teaching on discernment. By learning from our past experience, we can forearm ourselves by unmasking the deceits of the evil one.

We can recognize three such deceits, myths which

the devil has tried to pass off on the people of God as genuine obstacles to lay spirituality. The first of these we have already noted: Holiness is only for religious and priests. The church never really believed this, and in fact explicitly repudiated it in Vatican II. But as with all the devil's deceits, a half-truth lies at the heart of this myth. Holiness *is* difficult in the lay life. But it is no less difficult in the religious life. One does not clear the path to heaven merely by taking vows or by withdrawing to the cloister.

In truth, each way of life—the religious and the lay— has its own strengths and its own weaknesses. The celibate is free to devote herself or himself to the Lord's affairs; all he or she need worry about is pleasing the Lord (cf 1 Cor 7:32,34). This is indeed a beautiful advantage of the celibate life. But it is not an unmixed or automatic blessing. It is very easy for one who is unmarried to become concerned not about what pleases the Lord but about creating a nice, comfortable, undisturbed world for herself or himself.

Similarly, one who is married may not be distracted thereby from the Lord but rather purified for him by the demands of a good marriage. Married people have to take on a responsibility for another person in an exclusive way that celibates do not, which can reflect the loving fidelity of the Lord for his people. When I find a confrere in community irritating, or a community situation frustrating, I can go to my room and close my door. If I were married, I could not do that, because the problem is inside the room with me!

Maybe this balance of strength and weakness in both ways of life accounts for Paul's surprising admission in his teaching on celibacy: "Now concerning the unmarried, I have no command of the Lord, but I give my opinion as one who by the Lord's mercy is trustworthy" (1 Cor 7:25). He himself is called to celibacy, and can speak of its beauty and benefits from his own experience. But the

Lord is not prepared to reveal to Paul that what is best for him is best for everyone.

Another devil's myth which can disturb the lay person seeking to live a deep Christian life is that the world, in which the laity are called to be fully involved, is corrupting and hostile to any genuine spirituality. This was a major problem for the early Christians and for the New Testament writers. Jesus himself told his disciples: "If the world hates you, know that it has hated me before it hated you. If you were of the world, the world would love its own; but because you are not of the world, but I chose you out of the world, therefore the world hates you" (Jn 15:18-19). And in his priestly prayer, Jesus says to the Father: "I am not praying for the world but for those whom thou hast given me, for they are thine. . . . they are not of the world, even as I am not of the world" (Jn 17:9,14).

It does seem that in some sense the world is at war with God, and that those who belong to Jesus are separated from *this* world. The devil's myth here makes us believe that the word *world* has only one sense and that this world is simply and unqualifiedly evil; that physical nature and human relationships are always and inevitably obstacles to spiritual growth. This myth has power over men and women even today. People still seek to escape to the desert or the monastery because they mistakenly believe that they cannot save their souls in the world.

Many of my ex-students have told me it was much easier to be committed Christians when they were still at the university. The business world, they complain, does not recognize and even actively opposes the values they were taught at school. In reply, I have to admit that it is more difficult to be truly Christian in the marketplace than it was in the hothouse environment of the university. Something similar, by the way, is true of the young sister leaving the relatively sheltered environment of the novi-

tiate to enter the demanding world of her active apostolate. But are the difficulties they encounter a call either to
escape from the marketplace or to despair? Or are they
rather a challenge to mature in their own faith and to
bring Christ into the marketplace? The devil would have
us believe the former, but Jesus' answer is the latter. He
petitions the Father: "I am not asking you to remove them
from the world, but to protect them from the evil one"(Jn
17:15). The very challenge of the world can be sandpaper
to polish the sanctity of those who seek to become perfect
disciples of Christ in the lay life.

A third devil's myth often discourages committed lay
Christians. They realize the need of good guidance if they
are to grow in their faith and love. Yet they find such
direction all but impossible to come by. By contrast, it
seems to them that religious and priests have many more
opportunities for spiritual guidance. Again this is only a
half-truth for two reasons. In the first place, religious and
priests also complain of the difficulty of finding good
spiritual direction. And secondly, while such direction is
not common neither is it impossible to find. It is incon-
ceivable that a God who is Love would ever call us to
holiness without providing the means to realize his call. If
he gives the desire, he *must* make possible the fulfillment
of that desire. To believe any less would be to deny his
goodness.

Conclusion

As is probably clear by now, while we will reflect on
the place of the clergy and religious in the post-Vatican II
church, the reader I have primarily in mind is the committed lay Christian, married or single, sincerely seeking a
spirituality suited to his or her marketplace vocation.
Although I discuss secular apostolates and covenant
communities in Chapter Eight, my focus is not on organized forms of lay spirituality. I would like to speak to the
lay person *as lay*—living and working in the world of

everyday realities, whose only organized spiritual community may be the family and the parish. It is this person to whom Vatican II addresses its magnificent discussion of the lay vocation, and its universal call to holiness.

People frequently ask me, Is there any such thing as a distinctive *lay* spirituality? Or is the spirituality of the laity simply the gospel spirituality proclaimed by Jesus and the New Testament writers? In essence, I would say, there is only one Christian spirituality. Every Christian is called to live the teaching of Jesus himself. As Saint Benedict said of his monks, the only real "rule" of life is the Sermon on the Mount.

None of us, however, can capture in our own lives the whole of the gospel message. We are finite. Like the Buddha's blind men grasping various parts of the elephant, each of us may be wholly in touch with the elephant and yet not embracing the whole elephant. Our spiritualities differ, not in essence but in the particular aspects of the Christ-life which they emphasize and highlight. Among religious communities, for example, Franciscans stress poverty and fraternity; Jesuits, obedience and discerning availability; Dominicans, sound doctrine. None denies the truth or importance of the others' emphases. Indeed, each needs the others to reveal the whole Christ. Similarly, I believe that the lay vocation has its own distinctive emphases and charisms. It is in this sense that we can speak of a specifically lay spirituality.

These distinctive emphases and charisms will become clear, I trust, in the pages to follow. Part One is historical, tracing in broad outline the gradual evolution, from the scriptures to the Second Vatican Council, of the church's understanding of the meaning and value of the lay vocation. Part Two is thematic. I consider the essential elements of any authentic Christian spirituality in Chapter Five, while the following chapters explore the implications

of the emerging "age of the laity" for the various particular vocations—religious life, the priesthood, marriage and
the single life—within the church. Finally Chapter Eight
discusses the role of community in lay spirituality.

This topic of lay spirituality has been germinating in
my mind for several years now. In the past two or three
years I have had occasion to speak about it, to write (most
recently in a series of articles in the Manila *Chronicle*), and
to ask others for suggested topics. One recurrent theme
has been this: to make clear that the Christian vocation is
above all a call to live joyously, that a true and mature
disciple of Jesus is a *happy* person, whatever difficulties or
sufferings life may bring. A holy person is necessarily a
happy person, courageous and trusting, because he or
she lives strong in the conviction that the Lord has truly
"overcome the world" (Jn 16:33). In the Epilogue we will
discuss this universal call to happiness as the heart and
goal of genuine lay spirituality.

I find it a real challenge to write about the lay life,
since it is not my own vocation. But my vocation *is* to
serve the people of God. I exist for them—for you. My life
would have little meaning and less fruit if I did not understand the needs and concerns and joys of those I serve.
Fortunately, I have had good teachers. From my parents I
first learned the beauty and the challenge of a good
marriage, and of a life lived honorably, justly and nobly
"in the world." My brother and sister (with their spouses)
as well as my many lay directees, single and married,
have continued my education.

In addition to acknowledging my sister, Pidge James,
for her valuable comments on the manuscript, and my
cousin Judy Parkes for her expert typing, perhaps I could
single out two couples to stand in for all of you: Remy
and Jess Ignacio, and Boy and Evelyn Nazareno. Remy
and Jess are a bit older than myself, while Evelyn and Boy
are half-a-generation younger. Both have large families,

one successfully raised and the other up and coming. Both have been pillars of the church in their (and my) Filipino parish, as well as my partners and co-workers in the barrio ministry there. Moreover, both couples have taken their faith as an inner and personal reality. They have recognized the need not only to do but to be—and have communicated this need to their children as well as to many others in their respective marketplaces. In dedicating this book to Jess and Remy, Boy and Evelyn, I dedicate it to all of you who share their life, and I thank you for what you have taught me about finding the Lord in all things.

♣ Part One

Historical Roots and Emergence

⚓ Chapter One

Coming to Terms With the "World"

Our Need for Roots

In attempting to understand the dignity and nobility of the lay vocation for a Christian, we are inevitably confronted with a doubt: If the lay person is truly called to holiness why have most lay people considered themselves to be second-class citizens in the church? It would be easy to say that they were victims of a clerico-religious conspiracy to keep them inferior. But it would also be false. The roots of the problem are much deeper and more complex than that. In order to understand better why the age of the laity has been so slow in coming in the church, we need to take a "bird's-eye" survey of early Christian history. What we can say is necessarily sketchy and incomplete, but it may suffice to help us understand our present situation better. We *are* our histories, and thus we can only understand today in the context of yesterday.

The common thread of our reflections in this book is the vocation of the lay Christian or Catholic to achieve the universal call to holiness which was one of the central themes of the Second Vatican Council. The hierarchy and the religious congregations still play an important role in the church, but not as superior to, more Christian, or holier than the people of God whom they serve. Indeed, *service* is the key word in understanding the hierarchical vision of the recent council. The tip of the pyramid (the papacy) exists not to lord it over the base (the laity) but rather—hence the image of the inverted pyramid—to be "the servant of the servants of God."

In the past century we have been blessed with an extraordinary series of popes. In the context of their times and cultures they have gradually moved the church closer to Jesus' own vision of apostolic authority. In Matthew's gospel Jesus tells his disciples:

> "You know that the rulers of the Gentiles lord it over them, and their great men exercise authority over them. It shall not be so among you; but whoever would be great among you must be your servant, and whoever would be first among you must be your slave; even as the Son of man came not to be served but to serve" (Mt 20:25-28).

And he said at the Last Supper,

> "You call me Teacher and Lord; and you are right, for so I am. If I then, your Lord and Teacher, have washed your feet, you also ought to wash one another's feet. For I have given you an example, that you also should do as I have done to you. Truly, truly I say to you, a servant is not greater than his master; nor is he who is sent greater than he who sent him" (Jn 13:13-16).

Since this was Jesus' own teaching on authority in the church, the great saints of every age have understood it and tried to live by it. In Chapter Six we will call as witnesses Saint Augustine, Saint Gregory the Great, and some more recent spiritual masters to show that the inverted pyramid of Vatican II is solidly rooted in the best of church tradition, and to testify to the hierarchy's proper role in and of the church. Both Gregory and Augustine saw their episcopal status more as a danger than a privilege. And, considering the challenges which confront a dedicated bishop in our own day, we can well appreciate their thinking. I believe that one of the reasons why we Catholics, in the eucharistic prayer of every Mass, pray for the pope and our bishop is not because they are privileged characters in the church, but rather because of the vulnerability of their position. Indeed, St. John of the Cross tells us that the devil will work more, not less, to seduce the leaders of the church, for if he can lead them astray, he can harm many others through their bad example.

It is noteworthy, though, that St. Gregory, in recounting the hazards of his position as pope, does not see the *lay* life as the ideal alternative. Rather, as we shall see in Chapter Six, he dreams of the peace and order of the *monastery* from which he came. To understand why this is so, we need to spend a bit more time considering the early days of the church. In so doing, we will find that Gregory's longing for monastic solitude in A.D. 600 had strong roots in the preceding centuries. And we will understand better why the age of the laity, which I suggested earlier was inaugurated by Vatican II, has been so slow and late in coming to the church.

A Fundamental Problem: Is the World Good or Bad?

The central problem in developing a lay spirituality seems to be the relationship between a committed Christian and the secular world. The gospels themselves are ambivalent concerning the relationship of the created, material world to the redemptive plan of God in Jesus Christ. Since this ambivalence remains with us today, and since scripture is always the touchstone of our faith, it will be helpful to consider briefly the scriptural teaching on the subject.

In the New Testament "*kosmos* (world) is both a cosmological and a theological term" (John L. McKenzie, *Dictionary of the Bible*, p.942). It refers to the created universe, the material creation which came from God and which he found good in the Genesis account of creation. But in the theological sense, the world is "the scene of the process of salvation; it is not merely the scene but also one of the protagonists (actors) of the drama, for the world is mankind as fallen, as alienated from God and hostile to God and to Jesus Christ" (McKenzie, p. 943).

Since God made people free, it was possible for sin to enter the world and to infect not only the sinners but also the world in which they live. The authors of Genesis, in chapter three, were quite aware of the pervasive poison of sin in creation: Because of the fall of Adam and Eve, man was to wrest his living from the land by the sweat of his brow and woman was to know the anguish of childbirth.

These struggles and sufferings are meant to symbolize a larger picture: a good world gone awry because of the introduction of sin into the story. If people were not free, they would be unable to love—since true love can only be freely given. But if they are free to love, they are also free to reject love. Freedom to do and be good inevitably and necessarily entails freedom to do and be evil.

The ambiguity and even ambivalence toward the world in the New Testament comes in this theological sense. As material creation the world can only be good, since it comes from the creating hand of the all-good God. But when conceived as fallen and in need of redemption, the world is hostile to Jesus while still being the object of his redeeming love. He came into the world and yet he is not "of the world" (Jn 8:23). Indeed, "God loved the world so much that he sent his only begotten Son . . . not to be its judge but to be its savior" (Jn 3:16-17). John's gospel frequently explored this love-hate relationship between God and the world.

Paul's letters, too, reveal this ambivalence. For example, while he writes: "In Christ God was reconciling the world to himself" (2 Cor 5:19), he asks the Christians at Colossae: "Why do you live as if you still belonged to the world?" (Col 2:20). He advises the Corinthians to "deal with the world as though they had no dealings with it" (1 Cor 7:31).

This is just a sampling of the passages cited by Father McKenzie to show the tension in the New Testament understanding of the world. He also makes clear, however, that tension does not mean contradiction. As we shall see, we can derive a consistent faith vision of the world from the teaching of Jesus himself, Paul and the other New Testament writers. We must struggle to find the balance of Christ in our attitude toward the world in which we live. He came into the world to redeem it from its rejection of unconditional love. The church has had a long journey between this gospel vision and the acceptance and affirmation of Vatican II.

The Apostolic Church: The Selective Power of Martyrdom
      The church portrayed in the *Acts of the Apostles* was small, close-knit and strongly communal.

> Now the company of those who believed were of one heart and soul, and no one said that any of the things he possessed was his own, but they had everything in common. . . . There was not a needy person among them, for as many as were possessors of land or houses sold them, and brought the proceeds of what was sold and laid it at the apostles' feet; and distribution was made to each as had any need (Acts 4:32,34-35).

While we know from other passages, for example Acts 5:1-11, that the situation was not wholly idyllic, a beautiful, simple joy still radiates from Luke's account of the Pentecost church. In part this must have been because the memory of Jesus victorious over death was still very fresh in their minds and hearts. Moreover, the numerous signs worked by the Spirit through the apostles gave them strength and buoyed their enthusiasm. If we look at the whole picture of the early church's life, however, a more sobering reason accounts for the vitality of the apostolic community: Every member was a likely candidate for martyrdom.

The early church was a small "ghetto" in an essentially hostile society. For the first several decades, her center was in Jerusalem and Palestine. Most of the early Christians were Jewish, considered by their neighbors and compatriots as renegades and apostates. When persecution, aided by Paul's extraordinary zeal to evangelize the Gentiles, drove them from Palestine into the wide world, they still found themselves in a generally hostile environment. Tradition tells us that all the apostles except John were martyred, and their fate was shared by many Christians right up to the time of Constantine in the fourth century. To be a Christian was almost automatically to risk martyrdom.

This tragically unjust situation did have one beneficial aspect: The prospect of martyrdom kept the level of commitment high! Today in a country like the Philippines where almost everyone is Christian, it is easy to profess one's belief in Christ. But faith and commitment can be superficial when it costs very little to claim the name of Christian. Persecution and death are only for the serious, the heroic, those who are quite detached from this passing secular world.

Moreover, the early Christians believed that now that Jesus had come with salvation, the end of the world was imminent. Paul wrote to the Corinthian community, advising them to detach themselves from all secular things, for "the appointed time has grown very short; . . . the form of this world is passing away" (1 Cor 7:29,31; cf. 1 and 2 Thes). If the cost of discipleship is coupled with a general belief that the world is about to end, there is not much incentive to value life in the world.

The Price of Respectability: Flight From the World
    As time passed it seemed that the *parousia* or second

coming of Christ was not really imminent. And by the third century in Alexandria, Christianity became accepted and respectable, so that martyrdom was no longer a significant danger for believers. In fact, the Christians were now the leaders of the community, as they would be a century later in Rome.

This security and acceptance might seem, and indeed must have appeared to the Alexandrian Christians, to be a great blessing. They could now proclaim Christ openly and in security, and they could see the fruits of their proclamation in the rapid growth of the church. And yet they soon realized that success and tranquility brought their own problems. As George Lane, S.J., puts it in a fine, brief summary (*Christian Spirituality*, Argus Press, 1968, p. 12 and Loyola Chicago Press, 1984): "But when the period of martyrdom and persecutions was over, how could a person reach the pinnacle of Christian perfection? Martyrdom had been the ideal, and now there were no martyrs. One had to search for another ideal."

Once being a Christian becomes easy, what happens to the gospel ideal of perfection? Concretely, did the church convert Alexandria, or did Alexandria convert the church? It seemed to some dedicated souls that the church lost much of her vitality and fervor once she was accepted by the secular world around her. They feared she was in danger of being converted by the world rather than converting the world. The same danger is present today in a country like the Philippines that is overwhelmingly Christian and even Catholic. If our faith is not challenged, will it really be strong? If church and state are too comfortable and too close in their relationship to one another, can we really avoid mediocrity or being used for purposes that may be opposed to gospel teaching?

The Alexandrians found salvation in the hermit life, a flight from the urban world that seemed to threaten the church with its suffocating embrace. By renouncing the world and fleeing to the desert, they could give themselves wholeheartedly to living the gospel teaching of Jesus. In their writing and thinking, this flight from the world was interpreted as a "substitute martyrdom." By dying to all the enticements and snares of the secular world, and especially of the world in the church itself, they could reproduce symbolically in their own lives the heroic death of the martyrs for love of Christ.

We cannot help but be impressed by the idealism of the early hermits. They reveal what Father Lane calls a "captivating enthusiasm." But their spirituality does tend to be elitist. Like the Hinayana or Theravada Buddhism of Sri Lanka and Southeast Asia, the hermits present an ideal of holiness which is accessible to very few.

As they interpreted the gospels, the secular world was hostile to the designs of God, as the source of attachments which entangle the hearts of men and choke off true growth in holiness. Connected with this problem is the belief that the higher spirit of a person, the real self, is at war with one's lower, physical nature. The body and its concerns are a drag on one's best aspirations. One's true self can only be achieved by escaping from the flesh which imprisons it.

The desert and its spirituality produced many great figures like St. Anthony and St. Pachomius. But, as seems to be the norm in human affairs, it also generated its own problems. It seems to represent a step backward from the universal call to holiness that the gospels proclaim. If the gospel teaching of Jesus was demanding, the desert ideal seems almost impossible for all but a few. The desert tended to project an elitist vision of Christian perfection; very few men and women could, or were even disposed to, renounce the world in such a radical way. Today we realize that even Jesus himself, in his own human life, did not do so. (See Matthew 11:16-19, where he contrasts his own lifestyle with John the Baptist's much more austere way.) But at the time total renunciation seemed to be *the* way to perfect discipleship—a way which only an elite few could follow. It was as if we were to believe today that only cloistered monks and nuns could be full disciples of Jesus.

St. Benedict and the Christian's Need for Community

The great St. Benedict is known as the father of western monasticism. There were other, earlier giants of the monastic life in the East, like St. Basil and St. Gregory of Nyssa, but none had such an impact on the history of the church. Much of what we know of Benedict we learn from Gregory the Great. It seems that Benedict was born about the year 480 and died in 547. As a youth he studied in Rome and experienced the same revulsion as the desert fathers of Alexandria to the corruption and mediocrity he found there. And as they had done more than two centuries earlier, he fled the city to live as a hermit on Mount Subiaco.

Benedict's story, however, does not end in the desert. After a few years he began the gathering of disciples which was to fructify in the monastic order which bears his name. There were monks before him, even in Italy, but their life seems to have been characterized by the excesses and eccentricities that also plagued the solitary life of many of the hermits. Benedict realized that "it is not good for man to be alone" (Gn 2:18). But he also realized that the community should be well ordered and based upon a rule, which for him was Jesus' Sermon on the Mount. If the monks lived together simply and harmoniously, with an ordered rhythm of work, prayer and relaxation, they could reach the heights of Christian sanctity. Moderation and discretion were hallmarks of the great Benedictine ideal. By contrast with the excesses of penance and of prayer that he had observed, Benedict proposed a new ideal: Holiness did not consist in doing extraordinary things, but in doing the ordinary with great

love. It was not the deeds themselves but the love with
which they were done that was the test of true discipleship.

The monk's world was small and self-contained
within the monastery, "so that there may be no need for
the monks to go abroad, for this is not at all healthful for
their souls" (*The Holy Rule*, p. 85 in the St. Meinrad
edition of 1956). Nonetheless the vision of Benedict does
represent a turning away from the extreme anti-world
stance of many desert figures. We have *begun* the journey
toward a spirituality of the lay life.

Elements of Permanent Value

The purpose of our very brief survey of the evolution
of Christian spirituality is to understand better the historical roots of today's "age of the laity." While we have only
spoken thus far about important developments in the first
six centuries, perhaps it is already clear that the church is
a living, dynamic reality. Like everything living, she must
grow and change if she is not to die. She is continually
enriched with new experiences and new challenges in a
changing environment. And her ongoing reflection on
these experiences leads to a deeper understanding of her
own self-identity and of the God who has called her "out
of darkness into his own marvelous light." The church
seems to grow gradually and according to the laws of
human nature. For us the process may seem frustratingly
slow, but in God's eyes a thousand years are as a single
day.

In my course on apostolic spirituality, where I spend
some time on the historical evolution which we have been
discussing, I find it helpful to point out the way in which
each of the various movements of the past can be of
permanent value to us. Even though times and circumstances have changed greatly since then, we can still find
something of lasting importance in the spirituality of past
ages. This is the importance of tradition in the church.

Two features of the apostolic church's spirituality are especially important even now. The first is the central role of the experience of Jesus in our faith life. Our faith is not primarily intellectual assent to a body of doctrines, but commitment to a person, to Jesus as Lord. We believe not in something but in Someone. To the early church this was clear. In replacing Judas, the apostles had to choose someone who had "accompanied us during all the time that the Lord Jesus went in and out among us, beginning from the baptism of John until the day when he was taken up from us—one of these men must become with us a witness to his resurrection" (Acts 1:21-22).

Paul stands as the link between the original apostles and ourselves. He had not known the Lord in the flesh—in his public or his risen life before the Ascension. It was crucial for Paul to establish that his faith and his mission were not grounded merely on hearsay, on the reports of others:

> Paul an apostle—not from men nor through man, but through Jesus Christ and God the Father, who raised him from the dead—and all the brethren who are with me, to the churches of Galatia: . . . For I would have you know, brethren, that the gospel which was preached by me is not man's gospel nor was I taught it, but it came through a revelation of Jesus Christ (Gal 1:1-2,11-12).

While not all of us are called to be apostles in the same way Paul was, we are all called to witness to our faith. This is the second element of the apostolic age's spirituality which is still important for us today. We are not, most of us, called to die for our faith as many of the early Christians were. But the original Greek word for martyr is witness. A martyr gives testimony to his or her faith in the Lord. Whether that testimony be in blood or in word or in good works, all genuine faith entails a martyrdom. And like the early Christians what we wit-

ness to is our personal experience of Jesus Christ and of
the Father whom he reveals to us.

If I had to choose one element of permanent value in
the Alexandrian flight to the desert, it would be what
Lane calls the "captivating enthusiasm" of the great desert
fathers. They may have slipped into eccentric ascetical
practices at times, their attitude toward the world may
have been excessively negative and anti-apostolic, but one
can only admire their singleminded passion for God. Any
Christian spirituality will only be authentically Christian if
it shares this passion.

Ignatius Loyola, one of the most apostolic of saints,
tells us in his *Spiritual Exercises* that the single *end* of our
lives is the glory of God and our salvation, and that
everything else must be seen as a means to this end. Such
singlemindedness is demanding and even intimidating,
but it is clearly the way of Jesus himself, especially in his
confrontation with the Pharisees in John's gospel (chapters
5, 7 and 8).

When we consider the great Benedict, I would
choose as most significant his stress on common life. This
was a reaction to the eccentricities of the desert, eremeti-
cal life, but it goes to the very heart of the gospel message. For Benedict, holiness did not consist in doing
extraordinary things—extreme fasting, unusual devotions,
long prayers—but in doing the ordinary with extraordinary love. This, again, was Jesus' own way. Calvary was
indeed extraordinary; so were his miracles. But the general tenor of his life was quite ordinary as he tells us
himself (Mt 11:18-19). He came "eating and drinking . . .
a friend of tax collectors and sinners." It was John the
Baptist who "came neither eating nor drinking," like the
fathers of the desert. Jesus taught a new, ordinary way.
Benedict made this clear to the church.

One other striking and valuable feature of the desert
and monastic movements we have discussed here is that

they were essentially lay movements. That is, they were
not initiated by, nor primarily intended for, the clergy. In
each monastery there would be one or more priests to
serve the needs of the community itself. But the vast
majority of members would be non-clerical or lay. On the
other hand, they were not lay in the sense that they lived
in the world, earning a living and raising a family. They
were different from both the clergy and the ordinary
Christians of their time. Like the clergy they were consecrated, set apart from the secular world to fulfill a sacred
function in the church; but, like the laity as we ordinarily
understand that term today, they were not part of the
church's official hierarchical structure.

The ambiguity about the meaning of the word *lay*
persists even to our own day. In the wake of Vatican II, for
example, the Trappists have returned to their lay Benedictine roots. And yet very few of us would think of the
Trappists as laymen in any ordinary sense. Similarly, the
last 50 years have seen a great flowering of secular institutes in the church—groups of men and women who take
vows and yet are not religious. First given official approval
by Pope Pius XII, they live in the world, dress and work
as do ordinary lay people, and often are not known to be
any different from their co-workers. And yet they *are*
different: They have vows of poverty, celibacy and obedience. They are lay, and yet they are not, at least not in the
ordinary sense of the word.

The emergence of the secular institutes in the church
coincides with the period of ferment leading up to the
Second Vatican Council. They represent a move away
from, or at least a new alternative to, the traditional forms
of apostolic religious life. And as such they foreshadow
the age of the laity which the council was to inaugurate.
To see more clearly, however, the significance of their
emergence, we need to look to our history again. We need
to see what happened to the lay character of early monas-

ticism and what forms of apostolic religious life were considered traditional by the early 20th century.

In Part Two of this book we shall consider how each of these elements of lasting value from our tradition applies to lay spirituality today. First, though, let us continue our survey of the gradual emergence of an apostolic spirituality in the church. We still have 1,500 years to journey from the monastic family of Benedict to the "age of the laity" of Vatican II.

♣ Chapter Two

Two Classic Models for an Apostolic Spirituality

Mission and Monastery: An Essential Tension

When Benedict turned away from the desert ideal of solitude and austerity, he made an important contribution to the church's understanding of the gospel ideal. His stress on living the gospel simply and joyfully and with moderation would lead eventually to the "universal call to holiness" of Vatican II's *Dogmatic Constitution on the Church*.

Benedict's inspired insight has become a part of all genuine gospel spirituality. Following Christ is never easy or undemanding. Jesus himself said, "Whoever does not bear his own cross and come after me cannot be my disciple" (Lk 14:27). And the Sermon on the Mount, which was for Benedict *the* "rule" of the monastic life, certainly requires generosity and total commitment of anyone who proposes to live by it. Benedict's essential point is that the total commitment of our love, not the grandeur of our works or the excess of our austerities, makes us true disciples of Jesus.

The Benedictine ideal spread rapidly in the years after his death. Many monasteries were founded as more and more Christians were attracted to the order, harmony and gospel simplicity of monastic life. Soon, however, a problem arose which indicated that Benedict's was not the last word in the history of Christian spirituality.

Gregory the Great, himself a Benedictine monk and abbot before he was elected pope in 595, heard reports of

the "angels" (*angeli,* English) of the north. When he
asked whether these fair-haired, vigorous tribes had been
evangelized, he learned that most of them had never yet
heard of Christ. To Gregory this seemed intolerable. But
whom could he send on this mission to preach the gospel? The diocesan clergy of the time were just beginning
to be bound to celibacy, but their commitment was to the
local church. The only alternative source of missionaries
was the monastery. Perhaps Gregory's own history as a
monk and an abbot predisposed him to choose the monks
for the evangelization of Northern Europe. In any event,
choose them he did—with momentous consequences for
the church and for the monastic life.

In conjunction with the already-existing monks of
Ireland, the Benedictines were enormously successful in
their work of spreading the gospel and Christian culture.
It was difficult, however, if not impossible, to combine
their missionary mandate with their monastic spirituality.
Benedictine life depended upon a regular ordered rhythm
of prayer and manual work (*"ora et labora"*). The former
included the chanting of the divine office and the conven-
tual Mass. While they affirmed the world much more
than the desert fathers had done, the monks' world was
still essentially self-contained, restricted to the small
fraternal community within the monastic walls. How
could one live such a life while proclaiming the gospel on
the highways and byways of Northern Europe?

In the end the tension between monastic spirituality
and missionary lifestyle led to the great reforms of Cluny
and Citeaux in the 10th to 12th centuries. These two
monasteries spearheaded what was essentially a "back to
the monastery" movement and an attempt to return to the
ideals of simplicity and community of Benedict himself.

The medieval reform and renewal of Benedictinism
bore fruit which has lasted even until now. The Citeaux
reform evolved into the Cistercians of the Strict Observ-

ance, our Trappists of today. But what of the missionary life of the church? The return to the monasteries, good as it may have been for the Benedictines themselves, left a vacuum in the church.

The Mendicant Call to Share Christ With Others

One thing should be clear enough already from our survey of the church's first millennium: God works slowly indeed! He seems to have a different sense of time from us mortals, whose span of life and activity is limited to 60 or 70 years. He does not seem to live in continual crisis as we do. Nor is this surprising if, as evolutionary theory tells us, this world of ours has been unfolding for billions of years already. The Lord, it seems, took an unimaginably long time even to get to the point of his creation—to create the human race as the crowning glory of his work. Perhaps, then, it is not surprising that the full apostolic meaning of the good news of Jesus has also been revealed to the church only very slowly.

Another feature of evolution is also helpful to our present reflection. Paradoxically when a new evolutionary breakthrough occurs, it seems to happen in several places simultaneously. When the time and the climate is right, new answers to changed conditions and needs erupt not once but several times. And so it was in our story. As the Benedictines returned to the monastic ideal of St. Benedict, medieval society was evolving rapidly. Urbanization, the development of a money (and not just a barter) economy, the emergence of nation states and diverse national languages in Europe, the rise of the first great medieval universities, even the ultimately unsuccessful crusades to recapture the Holy Land for Christianity—all of these factors combined to create a new climate of challenge and opportunity for the church.

One of the central questions of this challenge was: If it was not the proper charism of the Benedictines to evangelize the world, to whom did the task belong? The

late 12th and early 13th centuries saw the emergence of
what came to be known as the *mendicant* (begging) orders:
the Franciscans, the Dominicans, the Augustinians, and
even the Carmelites, once the failure of the crusades
drove them from the solitude of Mount Carmel in Palestine to refuge in France. They weren't professional beggars
in our sense today, but by contrast with the stable, self-
contained life of the monasteries, they were to be free of
the demands of large institutions and of a self-sufficient
agricultural economy. The injunction of Jesus to the first
missionary disciples became central to their charism: "Go
your way; behold, I send you out as lambs in the midst of
wolves. Carry no purse, no bag, no sandals; . . . Whatever house you enter . . . remain in the same house,
eating and drinking what they provide, for the laborer
deserves his wages" (Lk 10:3-5, 7).

The two most famous founders of the mendicant
orders were St. Francis and St. Dominic, who knew one
another and died within a few years of each other in the
1220s. They were entirely different in temperament (as
Francis well realized when, Dominic tells us, he rejected
the latter's suggestion that they join forces and amalga-
mate their new communities). And yet Dominic, ever the
practical organizer, had a valid point: His and Francis's
movements *were* essentially similar, Spirit-inspired responses to the signs of their times. They were to be
apostolic and not cloistered. Their very charism was to
share with others the experience of God which grounded
their own lives. This attempt to blend the contemplative
(monastic) and active (apostolic) dimensions of their lives
was not without problems. But it was the first real attempt to achieve such a blend, and the fruits are with us
still. Dominic, Francis and the other founders who shared
their vision live on today in the many men and women
shaped by their contemplative-apostolic charism.

The Spirituality of the "Mixed" Life

The early 13th century was a crucial moment in the unfolding of Christian spirituality. The great theologian of this time—and one of the greatest of all times—was St. Thomas Aquinas. We might say he was a second-generation Dominican, since he was born within a few years of Dominic's death. Thomas, as well as his Franciscan friend and fellow theologian St. Bonaventure, elaborated a theology of the mendicant life. It was, he said, a *mixed* life, a blend of the active and the contemplative. As such, it was a *higher* form of life than the purely contemplative.

While today we would not normally share the medieval fondness for ranking ways of life as higher and lower, superior and inferior, Thomas' statement is significant for two reasons. First, it goes against the traditional understanding of the contemplative, cloistered life as the most perfect way of following Christ. In so doing, it implicitly affirms that the world is not merely an obstacle to Christian perfection, to be renounced and fled from if one truly desires holiness.

Second, Thomas says, "Just as it is better to illuminate than merely to shine, so to pass on what one has contemplated is better than merely to contemplate." This statement from the *Summa Theologiae* (II–II, 188, a.6) was to have great influence in succeeding centuries. The one who prays and then shares with others the fruits of his or her prayer is like a candle or a lamp which sheds its light on others and does not merely glorify God in solitary splendor.

In such a spirituality, the apostolic life is the overflow of the contemplative. One goes first to the chapel, as it were, to be filled with God, and then goes to the marketplace to share with others the God he has encountered in prayer. One could, and Thomas did, appeal to the example of Jesus here. In the gospels, he withdrew to pray

before important decisions or actions in his life, for example Luke 4:42; 6:12; 9:10; and especially the 40 days in the
desert which inaugurated his public ministry (Lk 4:42),
and his agony in the garden (Lk 22:39-46) which strengthened him to face his passion and death.

Not only was prayer very important in Jesus' life, but
it was intimately linked to action. For him and for his true
disciples, prayer was not an escape nor an inward-turned
"navel gazing"—it was essentially connected to living out
the Father's will in action. Both St. Teresa of Avila and St.
Therese of Lisieux, cloistered contemplatives though they
were, were profoundly aware of this essential link. In our
day, too, any charismatic prayer community which is
solidly rooted in the gospel is concerned about the out-
reach or overflow of their times of prayer together.

Finding God in Others

From what we have seen of the church's history, it
seems that each great breakthrough in spirituality also
raises new problems for the future. The problem that
arose in the centuries after Thomas was the balance
between contemplation and action in a "mixed" life. In
theory, contemplation was still the heart of the matter.
Action, the apostolic involvement of the mendicants, was
an overflow of their prayer and drew its value from its link
to prayer. The mendicants were still essentially monastic
in their spirituality. For some, like the Rhineland mystics
(Tauler, Henry Suso, Ruysbroeck, et al.), the ideal was
still essentially contemplative; their most proper work was
to form other contemplatives.

In practice, however, most eventually chose to stress
action. By the time Martin Luther became an Augustinian
in the early 16th century, relatively few of his mendicant
brethren possessed the spirit of prayer which animated
Francis and Dominic, Thomas and Bonaventure.

From one perspective, the crisis in religious life in
the early 16th century led to tragic results. The one body

of Christ was divided into Protestants and Catholics and has continued to divide and subdivide down to our own day. While the tragedy of this division cannot be denied, we can also say that—as in earlier moments in the church's history—the crisis of the early 16th century also occasioned great breakthroughs. The Protestant Reformation led to a renewed sense of, and love for, scripture. And the Catholic Counter Reformation inaugurated by the Council of Trent led to a renewed and reinvigorated faith life within the Catholic church. Of greatest interest to us in this book, the religious crisis of the 16th century also led to the next great breakthrough in the church's understanding of gospel spirituality in the Christian life.

As in the 13th century, this breakthrough occurred to several people almost simultaneously. St. Angela Merici founded the Ursulines; St. Philip Neri, the Oratorians; St. Cajetan and Cardinal Caraffa (later Pope Paul IV), the Theatines; St. Ignatius Loyola, the Jesuits. What was the new vision which animated and united these great religious founders? Ignatius captures the essence of this new vision. He exhorted his Jesuits to seek God in all things (*"ut in omnibus quaerant Deum"*), and one of his most trusted followers described the ideal Ignatian apostle as a "contemplative in action."

To see the radical newness of the ideal here proposed, note that it is no longer a question of a partly contemplative and partly active life. We might say Ignatius suggests that we break down the wall between the chapel and the marketplace, seeking God in the latter as well as in the former. Realized in actual practice, this ideal would mean that we can pray always—in work as well as in formal prayer. The whole world would be "charged with the grandeur of God," in the words of the great Jesuit poet, Gerard Manley Hopkins.

The fully apostolic communities founded in the 16th century held the ideal of "finding Christ in the world." We share with others the Christ we have found in prayer, but we also *receive* from them the Christ they have found. God is truly present in our world. We no longer find him by looking away from our world and out to the heavens, but within the concrete circumstances of our ordinary human life.

Ignatius and the other great founders of apostolic communities were not naive. They realized full well the biblical ambivalence of the world—that it could speak in the voice of "the world, the flesh and the devil" as well as in the voice of God. That is why discernment—an art learned only by faithful prayer and long practice—is central to the Ignatian apostolic vision and formation. If we are to distinguish the voice of God from the seductive voices which lead us away from him, we must be truly discerning men and women. Nonetheless, we find a new optimism here: The world is no longer only the place where we *bring* God; he is already there, to be found by those who have the eyes to see. Zacchaeus, despite his small stature, does not have to climb the tree to see Jesus. He can do so right on the ground of his ordinary life!

The Real Meaning of Christmas

In the Old Testament, as one noted scripture scholar[1] has put it, Yahweh was revealed as "the God who acts" in the history of his people. History itself came to be central to the Judaeo-Christian tradition in a way it had never been before. Yahweh had a design for his people which was to be worked out in time and space.

With the coming of Jesus Christ into the world, this Jewish sense of the importance of history was deepened and even transformed. He was recognized by the early Christians as the longed-for Messiah of Isaiah: "Therefore the Lord himself will give you a sign. A young woman

---

[1] G. Ernest Wright, written with Reginald Fuller, *The Book of the Acts of God* (Middlesex, England: Penguin Books, 1965), pp. 16-22).

shall conceive and bear a son, and shall call his name Immanu-el" (Is 7:14).

Immanuel means "God is with us." The Jews understood it to mean that God would raise up for them a royal, prophetic leader who would be his instrument in leading them to freedom and holiness. But Jesus revealed himself as Immanuel in a much more radical, literal sense. He was not merely the prophet of God but God himself, present and acting in the midst of his people. The history of men and women had become the history of God.

As I reflect on the history of Christian spirituality, it seems that it can be seen as a growing awareness of the full meaning of the Incarnation. During the Christmas season we are usually busy with many things, especially in the Philippines where Christmas is celebrated with a beauty and festivity unexcelled elsewhere. It is not unusual to hear complaints about the commercialization of the celebration and pleas to "put Christ back into Christmas." The desire to preserve, or to recapture, the proper religious meaning of the Nativity is good, of course. But our reflections in this chapter can lead us even deeper. Even when we do preserve the religious spirit of Christmas, it is possible that we do not grasp its full meaning. If we see the sacred and the secular as simply opposed to one another, we may not have grasped the full meaning of the Immanuel event. God is *with* us, part of our very history. The secular belongs to him too. It has taken 2,000 years for us to begin to grasp the truth that God is really with us in the most radical sense. We don't have to flee to the desert, or even withdraw to the monastery in order to find him. Nor do we need to dichotomize our lives into separate times for encountering God and for coping with the world. He is present in the world for those who have the eyes to see.

♣ Chapter Three

St. Francis de Sales and the Devout Life of the Laity

A Spirituality for the Lay Life

St. Francis de Sales was born in 1567 (11 years after the death of St. Ignatius Loyola) in Savoy, was educated by the Jesuits in Paris from 1580 to 1588, and took a doctorate in law at Padua in Italy in 1592. He was a member of the nobility, and a friend of King Henry IV of France and of Pope Clement VIII. Francis was also a man of profound piety, ordained as a diocesan priest in 1593 and then appointed coadjutor bishop of Geneva to reform the church in the spirit of the recently concluded Council of Trent. He succeeded to the bishopric of Geneva in 1602 at the young age of 35.

Francis de Sales was a remarkable man, far ahead of his time. In 1604 he became the spiritual director of St. Jane Frances de Chantal, and in 1610 they founded the Institute of the Visitation, one of the first apostolic communities of women in the church. His dream that the Visitation nuns be truly "in the world" was thwarted by the contemporary bias that every woman, to be safe, must have *"aut virum aut murum"* (either a man or a cloister wall). Only long after the death of Francis de Sales and Jane Frances de Chantal would it be possible for religious women to live the fully apostolic life which Ignatius Loyola and others had instituted for men religious.

Another instance of Francis de Sales' originality

and creative vision is important for our study: He wrote
what is perhaps the first book on lay spirituality in the
history of the Catholic church, the *Introduction to the
Devout Life*. De Sales says in his preface:

> Almost all those who have hitherto written about
> devotion have been concerned with instructing persons
> wholly withdrawn from the world, or have at least
> taught a kind of devotion that leads to such complete
> retirement. My purpose is to instruct those who live in
> towns, within families, or at court, and by their state
> of life are obliged to live an ordinary life as to outward
> appearances. Frequently, on the pretext of some
> supposed impossibility, they will not even think of
> undertaking a devout life.

Even today I often encounter the difficulty Francis here
confronts. Lay men and women feel devotion is only
possible for religious and priests. De Sales sets out in the
Introduction to the Devout Life to prove them wrong.

He divides the work into five parts, providing a
practical and methodological approach to holiness in the
world. He addresses the work to "Philothea, since I wish
to direct what was first written for one person alone to
the general benefit of many souls: hence I use a name
that can refer to all who aspire to devotion. 'Philothea'
refers to a soul loving, or in love with, God."

While Francis is convinced that true and solid spirituality is possible for the lay person living in the world, he
stresses that the basic prerequisite is a genuine desire to
love God. We might add that the same is true of a religious or priest. The Lord never forces himself on anyone.
He solicits, knocks at the door, but can only enter our
lives if we freely open the door to him (Rv 3:20). For those
who do truly desire to learn to love God—and that is
what holiness really means—Francis provides a step-by-
step discussion of the way to fulfill that desire in the lay
life.

"In the first part," he tells us in the preface, "by warning against certain things that need correction, and by certain exercises, I try to change Philothea's simple desire into a solid resolution." The nature of devotion, which is the perfection of charity, "not only makes us prompt, active and faithful in observance of God's commands, but in addition it arouses us to do lovingly and quickly as many good works as possible." As Ignatius and Teresa of Avila had said, love consists not so much in words but in deeds.

Francis further warns us that a good director is important if we are sincere in our desire to grow. "Do you seriously wish to travel the road to devotion? If so, look for a good man to guide and lead you. This is the most important of all words of advice" (Part I, chapter 4). He realizes that such a guide is not easy to find, but he insists that the Lord will provide for those who are sincere in their desire to grow, and who perseveringly beg him to give them "a good and faithful guide."

In our day good spiritual directors are still not easy to find. But we do have one advantage which earlier ages lacked: Many good books are available to help fill the void. Classics like the *Introduction to the Devout Life* have been translated into countless languages and are available in inexpensive editions. And many contemporary masters like Anthony Bloom, Rosemary Haughton, Thomas Merton and Caryl Houselander help us relate the Christian spiritual tradition to the needs and conditions of our own day.

Laying a Good Foundation

Assuming that Philothea, moved by her desire for God, has found a good guide for her journey, how does she begin? For Francis de Sales, writing in 1609, the answer was clear.

Once we do desire to be serious about God and to live a good and prayerful life, we must first purify our

soul of sin and of its sinful attachments. This is the solid
foundation required for any genuine Christian spirituality.
Francis tells the beginner that he or she should make a
good general confession and then "a firm protestation,
followed by Holy Communion, in which she gives herself
up to her Savior and happily enters into his holy love."
Most of part I of his *Introduction to the Devout Life* concerns this need for conversion and initial purification. He
suggests nine meditations, on topics such as creation, sin,
death and the last judgment to help us to this purification. Ignatius suggests similar topics for meditations in
the first part of his *Spiritual Exercises*, but Francis adapts
the meditations to the specific situation of the layperson.
Today we are blessed with many means to achieve a
conversion of heart, such as the Cursillo, charismatic Life
in the Spirit seminars, and Marriage Encounter. Also
more and more retreat houses throughout the world offer
lay men and women the opportunity for a good retreat
along the lines recommended by Francis de Sales.

In the second part of the *Introduction to the Devout Life*
Francis teaches Philothea how to build on the good
foundation already laid. Like all the masters of prayer, he
is well aware of the danger that our conversion may be, as
we say in the Philippines, *ningas kugon*. That is, like the
field grass, it burns with intense heat at the beginning
only to die out very quickly. It is easy to make a good and
fervent cursillo or weekend retreat and then find ourselves, after some months or even weeks, worse off than
we were before our conversion. Jesus himself warned us
of this danger:

> "When the unclean spirit has gone out of a man, he
> passes through waterless places seeking rest, and
> finding none, he says 'I will return to my house from
> which I came.' And when he comes he finds it swept
> and put in order. Then he goes and brings seven other

spirits more evil than himself, and they enter and
dwell there, and the last state of that man becomes
worse than the first" (Lk 11:24-26).

How can we fill the house with the Good Spirit, so
that the evil spirits will find no vacuum when they seek to
return? For Francis de Sales the two great means are "the
sacraments, by which God comes to us, and holy prayer,
by which he attracts us to himself." He treats of prayer
first in part II, and lays greatest stress on what has been
called mental or meditative prayer. This corresponds to
the "getting to know" stage I discussed in *Opening to God*
(Ave Maria Press, 1977). While aspirations and formula
prayers are also helpful, we need to *listen* to God and not
merely talk to him. We do this listening first of all by
means of the scriptures.

Francis discusses the preparation for listening prayer,
the actual prayer itself, and various supplementary exercises like the morning offering of the day and the evening
examination of conscience. He lays great stress on the
preparation, convinced that being properly prepared to
encounter God is at least half the battle. The preparation
"consists in two points: (1) place yourself in the presence
of God, and (2) invoke his assistance." In chapter 2 of part
II he suggests various means for achieving "a lively,
attentive realization of God's absolute presence," and in
chapter 3 he suggests how we can ask the Lord for what
we seek in this time of listening prayer. It may be some
particular grace or insight we need today, or it may be the
general grace to know, love and follow him more gener-
ously.

The remaining chapters of part II discuss other
means to grow in the devout life. In chapter 12, de Sales
speaks of a spiritual retreat as "one of the most certain
means to spiritual advancement," which will lead him
later (part V) to extol the great value of an annual retreat,
now not for the purpose of initial conversion as above,

but to continue to grow in and deepen our committed love of God. And in the concluding chapters of part II he sees the Eucharist and confession as privileged means to this same end. Chapter 14 urges Philothea, as I have done with every directee of mine who sincerely desired to grow in God's love, to "make every effort to assist every day at Holy Mass," while chapter 19 recommends weekly confession, even if there is no grave sin, as a very fruitful way to "practice the virtues of humility, sincerity, obedience and charity."

In studying the program for a devout lay life which Francis de Sales presented some 380 years ago, what strikes me first is the familiarity, the ordinariness of what he proposes. Even today I recommend essentially the same regimen to anyone desirous of laying a sound spiritual foundation. A genuine conversion experience, such as a good retreat can provide, is still necessary for one beginning a devout life. John the Baptist's preaching of repentance must always prepare the way for the coming of the Lord into our lives. Moreover, this good foundation is not the whole building. We must build upon it with a daily, ongoing program of meditative prayer, consciousness examen, good works and frequent reception of the Eucharist and of the sacrament of reconciliation. There are no magic formulas, no short cuts to holiness. I would be just as sure of that today as Francis de Sales was in 1609.

Equally striking, and much more original, is his conviction that such a committed, deep Christian life is possible for the ordinary lay person. De Sales was a pioneer in the area of lay spirituality. His originality lay not in the plan he proposed but in his conviction that it was realistic and livable even in the midst of the distractions of the marketplace.

Is the Devout Life Really Possible for the Laity Today?
Francis de Sales insists that his directees were able to

follow, and profit from, the spiritual regimen he proposes in his book. But we can still ask whether it is really possible for the committed lay Christian *today*. He seems to have had in mind a person of some education, even a member of the nobility or upper, leisured class. Since printed books were still relatively rare in his day, his readers were likely to come from this class of society. What then of the ordinary person today—one who is sincere in his or her faith but has to work hard to earn a living or raise a family? Can the laity, too, follow the program of spirituality proposed by Francis de Sales?

I think they can, provided they possess the balance and common sense so characteristic of Francis himself. He was keenly aware of the need for a healthy realism in our pursuit of the love of God. He stresses that beginners should not be too ambitious:

> While blessing God for the supereminence of others, let us keep to our lower but safer way. It is less excellent but better suited to our lack and littleness. If we conduct ourselves with humility and good faith in this, God will raise us up to heights that are truly great (part III, chapter 2).

With the help of a good director and with common sense—seasoned by that best of all senses of humor, the ability to laugh at ourselves—we can begin the journey to the love of God from where we are right now. If daily Mass is not possible while the children are small, I can begin with what *is* possible and hope for more when the children are grown. I can find the pattern of confession most suited to my own person and needs: If I am scrupulous, once a week might be too often, but if I tend to be easygoing and self-indulgent, it might indeed be good to confess weekly. The challenge is to find the pattern or frequency which most helps me to growth and peace of soul.

In discussing the virtues proper to the lay life, St.

Francis de Sales is equally down-to-earth and realistic. He
begins with patience, humility, a proper concern for our
financial affairs, obedience, chastity (especially as this
virtue applies to the married state), and poverty of spirit.
On the latter topic he has two chapters which are entitled
"How to Practice Genuine Poverty Although Really Rich"
and "How to Practice Richness of Spirit in Real Poverty."
Francis wants us to ground our holiness in our own
concrete life situation. Similarly, in his earlier discussion
of humility, he has a chapter entitled "How We Are to
Preserve Our Good Name While Practicing Humility." He
is a great exponent of a balanced middle way between
extremes.

While most of the virtues are treated in one or two
chapters each, St. Francis devotes six chapters to humility,
six to friendship, and five to speech and our judgment of
others. The first two remind me of St. Teresa of Avila,
who had died about 25 years earlier and whom he refers
to several times though she was not yet canonized. For
Teresa, humility was the foundational virtue for all genuine holiness. But she did not understand humility as self-
deprecation or a poor self-image. For her, humility is
truth: The humble person knows that everything is gift,
since he has a clear and truthful knowledge of who God
is and who he is.

Friendship was also important in Teresa's program of
holiness. She says, in effect, if you wish to grow in the
love of God choose your friends accordingly. How many
youths have almost ruined their lives because of their
companions? But how many others have become good
partly because they were so blessed in the friends they
had? What Francis de Sales has to say about the sins and
virtues of the tongue is closely connected to the topic of
friendship, as is his discussion of legitimate "games" and
amusements. Today movies, dancing and social drinking
might have to replace the amusements he knew in his

day, but the principles of balance and moderation would
still be fully relevant.

Part III concludes with a beautiful discussion of
marriage, virginity and widowhood. De Sales spends
more time on marriage than on the other two, since most
lay adults spend most of their lives in the married state.
As we would expect by now, he treats marriage very
positively, as one of God's greatest gifts, balancing the
rights and joys against the obligations of marriage.

> Above all else I exhort married people to have that
> mutual love which the Holy Spirit in Scripture so
> highly recommends to them. . . . It was God too, my
> friends, who with an unseen hand tied your holy
> marriage bond and gave you to one another. Why then
> do you not cherish each other? (chapter 38).

Francis's treatment of marriage is somewhat brief. But
even here he provides a model, especially for celibates like
me. Chapter 39 is entitled "The Sanctity of the Marriage
Bed." He says that sexual pleasure and eating are both
appetites of the flesh and thus somewhat similar. So, "I
will try to explain what I cannot say about sexual pleasure
by what I say of the other." How much closer to God we
would all be if we spoke of what *we* know—and avoided
pontificating out of our ignorance!

The Challenges of the Lay Life

In part IV Francis discusses the "most frequent
temptations" which the devout layperson is likely to
encounter. As always, we will find him strikingly down-
to-earth and surprisingly relevant even today. He begins
by warning us that "We must disregard the criticisms of
this world's children" (chapter 1). In his day as in ours,
those who become serious about and committed to God
will always encounter misunderstanding and even criticism. Sometimes this will be due to envy, or because our
practice of piety is a threat to others who know, deep

down in their hearts, that they themselves are not living
as they should. Jesus himself experienced this, first from
his own townspeople (Lk 4:16-30), and then from the
Pharisees.

Such opposition can be a truly difficult temptation,
especially for the beginner in the spiritual life. As we
mature we become more sure of ourselves and more
confident that God is truly working in us. But at the
beginning the world of the Spirit is still strange and
unfamiliar to us and we are more prone to be shaken by
the skepticism of those around us. Francis insists that we
need great courage and trust as we begin to live a devout
life. Good friends, for example a prayer group that shares
our new vision and values, a good director and good
reading are a real help, especially in the early stages.

Both beginners and the mature need to be aware of
the difference between temptations and sins. All of us are
tempted, and we will be until our last breath. Even the
saints have been tempted severely, as de Sales points out.
But a thousand temptations do not make one sin. Francis
outlines three stages to any temptation: "(1) sin is proposed to the soul; (2) it is either pleased or displeased by
this proposal; (3) finally, it either gives consent or it
refuses." The temptation proper is not sin—even Jesus was
tempted in this way. Surprisingly, the soul's reaction to
the temptation is also not sin if the pleasure is in our
lower, instinctual nature and not in our will. Only when
we freely consent to the temptation do we sin.

Since temptation is such a pervasive part of all of our
lives, Francis de Sales spends several chapters encourag-
ing the committed soul, and explaining to her how to
handle temptations. We must not panic but rather treat
them as a normal part of our lives; we must learn to turn
firmly from these temptations and not toy with them like
the moth hypnotized by the flame; we must acquire a
genuine self-knowledge that will make clear to us which

temptations we are most vulnerable to. Together with this self-knowledge, which I also discussed in chapter 5 of *Opening to God*, we must also practice some penance to strengthen our will in areas where we know ourselves to be particularly vulnerable to temptation.

What we must *not* do is allow ourselves to be consumed with anxiety. Francis says:

> With the single exception of sin, anxiety is the greatest evil that can happen to a soul. . . . Anxiety proceeds from an inordinate desire to be freed from a present evil or to acquire a hoped-for good. Yet there is nothing that tends more to increase evil and prevent enjoyment of good than to be disturbed and anxious (chapter 11).

In every Mass, after the Our Father, we pray "free us from sin and protect us from all anxiety." God is a God of peace and not of turmoil; anxiety is the devil's native air.

Our discussion of St. Francis de Sales' classic, the *Introduction to the Devout Life*, has barely scratched the surface of its riches. But we have seen enough to realize that a genuine lay spirituality is truly possible—not easy, but possible. To grow in the love of God is difficult in any state of life, whether priestly or religious or lay. It requires real commitment, great trust in God and sound balance and common sense. Because Francis de Sales possessed and taught all of these, he laid the groundwork for the age of the laity in our post-Vatican II church.

The Harvest of Francis de Sales

In the 300 years following its publication, the *Introduction to the Devout Life* was translated into virtually every major language and published in innumerable editions. Clearly, Francis touched a sensitive and responsive nerve in the church. Many lay Christians were evidently searching for a deeper, more personal, more meaningful spirituality. They found in de Sales a gentle but firm, optimistic and yet realistic guide for their journey to the heart of Christ.

In this chapter we have sought to get a feel for his teaching and his winning personality—and for the important role he played in the history of the church's spiritual evolution. He is, we might say, the bridge between the earlier emergence of an apostolic spirituality, in the 13th and 16th centuries, and the recent emergence of the age of the laity in the Second Vatican Council.

The influence of the Ignatian tradition in which he himself was formed is especially prominent in his *Introduction*, although he was open to all the riches of the Christian tradition. He in turn influenced profoundly the generations who came after him. Many spiritual writers would address the problem he formulated of a spirituality for the marketplace. While they could and did emphasize various aspects of Christian spirituality, for example, the Marian, the eucharistic, the trinitarian, the basic outline of an authentic following of Christ in the lay life was delineated by Francis de Sales.

Any sound Christian spirituality requires grace, commitment, perseverance, good sense and joyous hope. These, at least, are the words that come to my mind when I attempt to summarize the message to Philothea of St. Francis de Sales. His specific focus, of course, is the lay life: He is convinced that each of these five elements is fully realizable for one living in the world.

Grace is fundamental and all-important. The work of our sanctification is primarily God's work. He draws us to himself. The desire to know and to love him can only come from him—not from ourselves. Consequently, as I often have to tell my directees, if the desire to grow is present in our hearts that itself is a clear sign that God is at work. And he *never* implants the desire in us unless he intends to fulfill it. To believe otherwise would be to deny his goodness and wisdom. It is most important to stress this, especially in the lay life whose many challenges and temptations can make real growth in virtue seem (but only *seem*) impossible.

While grace is all-important, however, it is not the whole story. We must freely respond to the Lord's drawing. This is where Francis de Sales is an especially good guide. We might say that his whole book is a manual of instructions for one seeking to respond to God's gracious initiative. Commitment and perseverance are essential. The person who desires to live the devout life must, as de Sales insists, both begin well and persevere in the work well begun. Holiness, growth in the love of God, is the fruit of generous response and sustained fidelity.

Jesus also insisted on this in his own public life. As he told the rich young man (Matthew 19:16-22), the first condition for entering into eternal life is to "keep the commandments." And the final sermon of his public ministry in Matthew (chapters 24 and 25) is a sustained exhortation to vigilance and perseverance. The fig tree, the conscientious steward, the wise and foolish virgins, the talents, the sheep and the goats—all are parables intended to bring out the importance of fidelity "unto the end" to our call and our commitment.

Good sense and joyous hope provide an essential balance in living the devout life. After Jesus' encounter with the rich young man, the disciples are overwhelmed by the demands of the gospel call. "And Jesus said to his disciples, 'Truly I say to you, it will be hard for a rich man to enter the kingdom of heaven. Again I tell you, it is easier for a camel to go through the eye of a needle than for a rich man to enter the kingdom of God' " (Mt 19:23-24). The disciples realize the real implications of Jesus' statement: We are *all* "rich" in the sense that all of us have attachments to what we possess or to what we desire to possess that make commitment and perseverance virtually impossible. "When the disciples heard this they

were greatly astonished, saying, 'Who then can be saved?'
But Jesus looked at them and said to them, 'With men
this is impossible, but with God all things are possible' "
(Mt 19:25-26).

For God everything is possible! This is the faith
foundation of the good sense and joyous hope so prominent in Francis de Sales. We do not have to have a ner-
vous breakdown in the pursuit of holiness. We do have to
do our part to cooperate and respond, but we do not have
to do God's part of the work. Nor should we think of him
as some aloof taskmaster, who sets standards for us and
then coolly sits back to see whether we fulfill them. He is
dying (has already died!) to unite us to himself. This is
the ground of Paul's joyous hope in his letter to the
Romans: "What then shall we say to this? If God is for us,
who is against us?" (Rom 8:31). Francis de Sales realized,
as did Paul, that it could not be God himself, nor Christ
Jesus, nor the principalities and powers—nothing on earth
or in heaven or under the earth. This is why he is a firm
but gentle spiritual director and, like every great director,
a prophet of exultant hope.

This is not to say that we should embrace the naive
humanism of the "noble savage" myth. Humanity is not
simply innately good. Sin is also a reality, as is human
blindness. That is why Francis de Sales stresses the
importance of a good guide and of a well-balanced program of spiritual discipline. Still God is truly here for
those who have the eyes to see. While a gloomy, sin-
obsessed Calvinism, and its Catholic cousin Jansenism,
will exert a strong influence on the centuries following
de Sales' great work, he has pointed out the correct path
for the church to take. In Vatican II, as we shall see in the
next chapter, St. Francis de Sales' incarnational optimism
will be vindicated and canonized. And an important
communitarian dimension will be added—one that it was
perhaps not possible to realize in his day.

⚜ Chapter Four

Vatican II and the Age of the Laity

Coming of Age

In the Introduction I suggested that the recent ecumenical council, Vatican II, inaugurated the age of the laity in the Catholic church. As I write these lines, the church is preparing for a synod in Rome, to be held in late 1987, on the role of the laity in the church today. The synod, of which there have been several in recent years, is a creation of the post-Vatican II church—an attempt to foster dialogue and collegiality among the members of the church and between the church and the world. As far as I know, this will be the first major gathering of the universal church devoted wholly to the topic of the laity. That fact itself is significant but perhaps not surprising in light of what we have seen thus far in this book.

In our historical survey of the progression of the church toward the age of the laity, we now come to the present day and the work of the Second Vatican Council. I would like to explore with you the essential vision of Vatican II, what the bishops refer to as the "universal call to holiness." It might be good, however, to provide just one more historical footnote as background.

The last church council before Vatican II was held in 1869-70, and was known as Vatican I. The councils are named from the place where they are held, and out of 21 generally recognized as official, "ecumenical" councils, only these last two were held in the Vatican. Vatican I

intended to do a comprehensive theology of the church in
the 19th century. But it was interrupted by the Franco-
Prussian war and was never able to reconvene. As a
result, those of us who grew up between Vatican I and
Vatican II had a top-heavy vision of the church. Vatican I
completed a strong document on the papacy, and a rather
strong treatment of the bishops' place in the church. But
they never were able to finish their work—with the result
that the other members of the church (clergy, religious
and laity) were not as clearly and strongly defined as were
the papacy or even the episcopacy. One hundred years
later, in Vatican II, the bishops finally arrived at a comprehensive vision of the church. We could say that this delay
was most unfortunate, especially for those of us whose
faith was formed in that century between 1870 and 1965.
But the vision of Vatican II on the laity could scarcely have
been enunciated in 1870 and renewal would still have
been necessary.

A Comprehensive Vision of the Church

The Second Vatican Council, the most recent general
council of the Catholic church, was held from 1962 to 1965
and brought together some 2,000 bishops from all over the
world—more than twice as many as attended Vatican I
earlier. The church had grown tremendously, both in
numbers and in geographical extent, over the preceding
century. And for the first time there were bishops of
virtually every race and color, and from all the inhabited
continents.

Pope John XXIII, who convened Vatican II, had
definite ideas concerning the kind of council that was
called for in our day. In the past, councils had been
convoked to settle doctrinal and jurisdictional disputes
within the church. "Good Pope John" had a different
vision for Vatican II: It was to be pastoral rather than
dogmatic in its approach. That is, it was intended to bring
the church into dialogue with the modern world and its

problems. The world had evolved rapidly, especially in the century since Vatican I. The new council, John XXIII believed, would be a golden opportunity for the church to understand this new world in the light of the gospel of Jesus Christ, and to explain herself and her mission to a world whose thought and culture were increasingly secularized.

No one except the Holy Spirit knew how the council, the largest gathering of Catholic bishops in history, would actually unfold. John XXIII himself died in June of 1963, after the first of the council's four sessions. His successor, Paul VI, the first pope in centuries to travel outside Europe and the first ever to visit the Orient, guided it to completion. In the end the council did realize the dream of John XXIII for an "aggiornamento" or renewal of the church in her own inner life and in her relationship to the modern world.

Like the Philippines' revolution in February, 1986, Vatican II did not solve all problems. In some ways it created more problems than it solved, but this was precisely because it set the church on a whole new course. It provided a new paradigm, a new way for the church to see herself and the world within which she fulfills her mission from Jesus Christ.

At the end of the council the bishops and the pope had approved 16 documents on a wide range of topics such as ecumenism, the liturgy, priestly formation, the missions, the apostolate of the laity and religious freedom. One remarkable document, entitled *The Church in the Modern World*, tackles a great variety of pressing current problems, from nuclear war, the United Nations and the relationship between the Third World and the industrialized world to such domestic concerns as family life and birth control.

The centerpiece, however, of the whole council is the *Dogmatic Constitution on the Church*, known officially as

Lumen Gentium from the first words of its Latin text. It
means "light of the nations," and the text in English
begins this way: "Christ is the light of all nations. Hence
this most sacred Synod, which has been gathered in the
Holy Spirit, eagerly desires to shed on all men that radi-
ance of His which brightens the countenance of the
Church. This it will do by proclaiming the gospel to every
creature" (No. 1).

These are the first words of Chapter 1, "The Mystery
of the Church." The reference to the church as mystery or
sacrament is reminiscent of St. Paul's use of these words
(Rom 16:25; Eph 1:9) to describe the saving plan of God
the Father, hidden from all eternity in his mind and only
now made manifest in Christ. Jesus Christ is the primor-
dial or fundamental sacrament of God's love for his
people, and the church is the extension of his human life,
until the end of the world. Thus she owes her origin not
to men but to God himself.

The Meaning and Mission of the Laity

In chapter 2, the council searches for a metaphor
which will most suitably describe the church to men and
women today. A likely candidate, popularized especially
by Pope Pius XII in the decades before Vatican II, was the
"mystical body of Christ." Indeed, the council frequently
uses this metaphor, since it expresses well the theme of
diversity in unity which is central to the council's vision.
St. Paul used the body metaphor to express the fact that
the church is made up of diverse members, each with its
proper role and none able to do without the other. "If the
whole body were an eye, where would be the hearing? If
the whole body were an ear, where would be the sense of
smell? . . . If all were a single organ, where would the
body be? As it is, there are many parts, yet one body" (1
Cor 12:17,19-20).

In the end, however, the council chose another
metaphor to express the church's nature: the people of

God. The idea is similar, but the "people of God" image, which echoes the description of Israel in the Old Testament, is sociological rather than biological. It brings out that the parts of the church are not *merely* parts—they remain unique individuals who *freely* come together to form a community.

The bishops cite several Old Testament passages to show the biblical roots of the people of God image; for example, "This is the covenant which I will make with the house of Israel after those days, says the Lord: I will put my law within them, and I will write it upon their hearts; and I will be their God, and they shall be my people" (Jer 31:33). They make clear that the metaphor is also significant in the New Testament, especially in the first epistle of Peter:

> But you are a chosen race, a royal priesthood, a holy
> nation, God's own people, that you may declare the
> wonderful deeds of him who called you out of
> darkness into his marvellous light. Once you were no
> people but now you are God's people; once you had
> not received mercy but now you have received mercy
> (1 Pt 2:9-10).

We are the people of God not only in the sense that we belong to him but because he has gathered us together and made us one. The church is the Lord's creation. Yet because we are a community or a society, we *freely* accept his call to become one in Christ. Unlike a physical body whose parts have no say in their belonging to the body, the people of God are united by their free choice to respond to the call of the Lord.

Granted that free response, however, we *are* like a physical body in that different members have different roles to play in the community. The council fathers continue their discussion in *Lumen Gentium* by examining the various roles played by different members of the people of God. Chapter 3 discusses the hierarchy, which in this context means the pope, bishops, priests and deacons. Chapter 4, which we will discuss in detail in the remaining sections of this chapter, treats of the laity; chapter 6 deals with the religious life (e.g., sisters and brothers); chapter 7 considers the church "beyond the grave," the communion of saints that links us to the souls in purgatory and the saints in heaven; chapter 8 provides a beautiful conclusion to the whole document with a discussion of the Blessed Virgin as a member, a model, and the mother of the church. We will return to chapters 7 and 8 in the Epilogue of this book.

Our primary concern here is with the laity, and so let us focus on chapter 4 of *Lumen Gentium* (to which chapter 5 is linked, since it deals with the "universal call to holiness" of all the members of the church). The council fathers begin their discussion in chapter 4 by defining the laity as "all the faithful except those in holy orders and those in a religious state sanctioned by the Church" (No. 31). So lay men and women are all those who are not ordained and are not members of religious congregations. But this definition is still quite negative. We may well ask, What *are* lay people? What is their proper and postive role in the church?

The council does try to answer that question, and in doing so provides us with an original and beautiful vision of what it means to be a lay Christian. It says that the laity

> are in their own way made sharers in the priestly, prophetic and kingly functions of Christ. They carry out their own part in the mission of the whole Christian people with respect to the Church and the world. A *secular quality is proper and special to laymen*. It is true that those who are ordained can at times engage in secular activities. . . . But the laity, *by their very vocation*, seek the kingdom of God by engaging in temporal affairs and by ordering them according to the plan of God (No. 31, my emphasis).

The Apostolate of the Laity

In the thinking of the church, the lay life is a vocation, a call from God to bring the presence and the good news of Christ to the very heart of the world, the realm of secular affairs. "They are called there by God so that by exercising their proper function and being led by the spirit of the gospel they can work for the sanctification of the world from within, in the manner of leaven [or yeast]" (No. 31). The allusion here is to one of the shortest of Jesus' parables of the kingdom of God: "The kingdom of heaven is like leaven which a woman took and hid in three measures of flour, till it was all leavened" (Mt 13:33).

The yeast is mixed with the flour. It accomplishes its leavening work secretly, from within—and so it is with the layperson. A priest or religious is a public, official witness to the gospel. When he or she is present, people recognize the church's presence. But the layperson works to bring Christ's presence to the world without being noticeably different from the world he or she seeks to convert. We might say that the priest is the baker working on the flour of the world and the layperson is the hidden leaven. Without the yeast the baker could never accomplish his task. Each needs the other.

By working quietly and often anonymously within the secular world, the laity

> can make Christ known to others, especially by the testimony of a life resplendent in faith, hope, and charity. The layman is closely involved in temporal affairs of every sort. It is therefore his special task to illumine and organize these affairs in such a way that they may always start out, develop and persist according to Christ's mind, to the praise of the Creator and the Redeemer (No. 31).

While often hidden and "ordinary," this work proper to the layperson is also difficult and challenging. Since the world is a mix of good and evil influences, the layperson

needs to be discerning as well as courageous. This requires the kind of solid interior life and faith commitment
which St. Francis de Sales taught to Philothea.

The lay vocation is proper to every lay Christian. It
can be accomplished by a laborer, a farmer, an executive, a
housewife, a patient in the hospital, a student in school.
Each can be the yeast in that part of the world where he
or she lives. But the council also recognizes the importance of more structured and visible lay apostolates to
which some laypeople may be called. *Lumen Gentium*
leaves to a separate document, which we will refer to in
Chapter Eight, the specific guidelines for corporate lay
apostolates. It merely affirms their importance to the
church:

> Besides this apostolate [i.e., the general call which we
> have discussed above], which pertains to absolutely
> every Christian, the laity can also be called in various
> ways to a more direct form of cooperation in the
> apostolate of the hierarchy. This was the case with
> certain men and women who assisted Paul the Apostle
> . . . (cf. Phil 4:3; Rom 16:3ff.). Further, laymen have
> the capacity to be deputed by the hierarchy to exercise
> certain church functions for a spiritual purpose (No.
> 33).

While a formally organized lay apostolate is one of
the most heartening signs of the emergence of the age of
the laity in the church, these organized, corporate, visible
works of the laity are still secondary to that anonymous,
hidden witness which is the apostolate of the yeast.
Whether because of age, family circumstance or other
reasons, not every lay man or woman can be involved in
corporate, institutional works. But everyone is called by
God to sanctify his or her small part of the secular world
by witnessing, by the very way he or she lives, to the
presence and concern of Jesus Christ.

The Layperson as Priest, Prophet and King

Clearly the Second Vatican Council saw the lay vocation as a genuine call from God to transform and sanctify the secular world of human existence. Since every authentic Christian vocation is a mission, the proper mission of the layperson is to convert the world from within. In developing their presentation of the lay vocation and mission, the bishops applied to the lay life the triple role of priest, prophet and king. These three roles have traditionally been used to describe the mission of Jesus himself and of the church's hierarchy. But Vatican II insists that they are also helpful in understanding more deeply the beauty of the lay vocation. Let us briefly consider each of them in turn.

The layperson, man or woman, has a *priestly* role because "besides intimately associating them with His life and His mission, Christ also gives them a share in His priestly function of offering spiritual worship for the glory of God and the salvation of men" (No. 34). This is not to deny the specific role of the ordained priest in offering the Holy Eucharist and administering the sacraments. But the council does ask us to widen our horizon, and to recognize the fact that all of us are called, in all the actions of our lives, to offer a pleasing sacrifice to God. Thus for the laity,

> all their works, prayers and apostolic endeavors, their ordinary married and family life, their daily labor, their mental and physical relaxation, if carried out in the Spirit, and even the hardships of life, if patiently borne—all of these become spiritual sacrifices acceptable to God through Jesus Christ (No. 34).

And, we are told, in the Holy Eucharist the priestly sacrifice of the laity is joined to the supreme sacrifice of Jesus as an act of worship most pleasing to God.

In addition to being a priest in this sense, the layperson also shares the *prophetic* role of Jesus. A prophet is one who speaks to men and women on behalf of God, a witness to the saving love of God, proclaiming to others the word which God has spoken. The prophet must be a person of prayer in order to hear the word of God and must have the courage to speak this word openly and fearlessly to others. We see this clearly in the lives of the great prophets like Moses, Isaiah, Jeremiah, John the Baptist and Jesus himself. But in what sense are ordinary lay people also prophets?

Vatican II says that Jesus has sent them "that the power of the gospel might shine forth in their daily family and social life" (No. 35). They witness by faith and hope and patience to the faithfulness of God who never abandons those who trust in him. They do this witnessing not only in word but even more in deed: "Let them not, then, hide this hope in the depths of their hearts, but even in the framework of secular life let them express it by a continual turning toward God" (No. 35). So many people tell me it is difficult, even impossible, to live a truly committed life in the midst of the world's concerns and temptations. I can reassure them that it is possible, by the grace of God. But I am not a layman, so my reassurance will never be fully convincing. They need real *lay* prophets—men and women who live the same life they do and by their own commitment and fidelity proclaim to others that one can be a true follower of Christ in the marketplace. That kind of witness is convincing and irrefutable!

Finally, the layperson is not only priest and prophet like Jesus, but also a *king*. He or she is called to master creation and thereby to manifest to the world that Jesus Christ is Lord of all that is. Nothing in the world—no occupation, no state of life, no joy or sorrow—is outside the kingdom of Christ.

The faithful, therefore, must learn the deepest
meaning and the value of all creation, and how to
relate it to the praise of God. They must assist one
another to live holier lives even in their daily
occupations. In this way the world is permeated by the
spirit of Christ and more effectively achieves its
purpose in justice, charity and peace. The laity have
the principal role in the universal fulfillment of this
purpose (No. 36).

This conquest of the world for Christ involves two
tasks, one perfecting and the other healing. Within the
sphere of their secular competence, the laity strive

so that by human labor, technical skill, and civic
culture created goods may be perfected for the benefit
of every last man according to the design of the
Creator and the light of His Word. . . . Let the laity
also by their combined efforts remedy any institutions
and conditions of the world which are customarily an
inducement to sin, so that all such things may be
conformed to the norms of justice and may favor the
practice of virtue rather than hinder it (No. 36).

So the true Christian layperson is priest, prophet and
king. It is a demanding but beautiful vocation. Perhaps lay
men and women in the past have not valued their vocation precisely because they have not really appreciated the
challenge it entails. Vatican II seeks to remedy this failing
in our vision of the church. To be a lay Catholic does not
mean merely going to Mass on Sunday and keeping the
commandments; it extends to every day of the week and
every secular activity.

A New Sense of Worth

While I do not know the actual intention of the
council fathers who composed *Lumen Gentium*, I find it
striking and significant that the discussion of the laity's
place in the church forms the centerpiece of the final text.

Of the eight chapters in *Lumen Gentium*, the middle two
treat explicitly of the role of the laity in the church and
their call to holiness. It would appear that, stylistically,
the council's theology of the lay life occupies the central
position in the most important document of Vatican II.
Perhaps this confirms my belief that the Holy Spirit's
principal work in the council has been to bring the church
into the age of the laity.

In some sense the movement toward full lay participation in the life of the church began long before Vatican
II, for example, with the Catholic Worker Movement,
Catholic Action, Christian Socialism, and even Pius X's
promotion, early in this century, of frequent communion
and a much earlier age for first communion. The council
provided a charter, a theology which situated all these
various movements and developments within the church's
evolving self-understanding. These grassroots developments were not only recognized and accepted by the
church, but they were integrated into her authentic and
authoritative understanding of the gospel revelation of
Jesus. In this sense we can see the council's work as the
end of a spirit-inspired process.

In another and deeper sense, however, it is just a
beginning. The council provides us with a vision, with
guidelines and principles for living the Christ-life into the
21st century. But the living out of that vision, the imple-
menting of those guidelines and principles, even the
discovery of their full and real meaning, is the challenge
for the post-Vatican II church. The developments of the
past 20 years would seem to make that clear. Some feel
that the council has settled everything, and that our task
now is simply to follow the letter of the new law. Others
feel the council did not go far enough in settling things to
their liking. But, if our brief overview of earlier ages in the
church's spiritual evolution is a reliable guide, Vatican II
must be seen as a spirit-inspired *moment* in an ongoing

process. The desert, monastic, mendicant and apostolic religious movements were all parts of the church's gradual appropriation of the full meaning of the incarnation. None of them was the last word, but neither was any of them a mistake.

Vatican II is part of the same divine process. It carries us one step further, one level deeper in our appreciation that God is Emmanuel, God With Us. It situates the vision of the great St. Francis de Sales in an ecclesial context. Although he wrote the first important treatise on lay spirituality, de Sales' focus seems to be on the sanctification of the *individual* "devout" soul. Vatican II provides a much stronger and clearer social context for the devout life of the laity.

The challenge for us today is to live out this new vision in the concrete circumstances of our lives. How can the devout layperson be priest, prophet and king in the late 20th century world? What does Zacchaeus *do* after his encounter with Jesus? In Part Two of this book I would like to reflect with you on these questions. I speak not as a lay man, but as a friend and director of many lay women and men, and as one whose whole vocation is to serve the people of God. Vatican II will provide us with several helpful guidelines, which we can supplement and spell out with reflection on our own experience.

In the end, though, the challenge is yours. Jesus said,

> "Every one who comes to me and hears my words and does them, I will show you what he is like: he is like a man building a house who dug deep, and laid the foundation upon rock; and when a flood arose, the stream broke against that house, and could not shake it, because it had been well built" (Lk 6:47-48).

Faith tells us Jesus still speaks to us today—through the council and in many other ways. Our challenge is to *act* on his words, and so to build our house on the Rock.

♣ *Part Two*
Various Ways to One End

♣ Chapter Five
Essential Elements of Any Gospel Spirituality

Incarnation and Epiphany: Knowing and Doing
The first great Sunday feast of every new year is Epiphany, the end of the Christmas season for most Christians. In some countries of the Eastern church, like Russia, it is an even bigger feast than Christmas. In the Philippines we call this day the feast of the three kings, because on this day we read Matthew's account of the visitors from the east who came to Bethlehem to worship the newborn king of the Jews. Matthew does not call them kings but simply "men from the east who studied the stars." Nor does he say that there were three of them. Christian tradition over the centuries has made them kings, said they were three because of Matthew's mention of three gifts and even given them names: Gaspar, Baltazar and Melchior. While all of these details are legendary, the very fact they have been embroidered upon the original account of Matthew shows how precious this story has been to Christians throughout the past 2,000 years.

From the earliest years the wise men from the east have symbolized the Gentiles, the non-Jewish people, to whom Jesus was sent, in the same way that the shepherds on Christmas night represented the Jews. Traditionally Epiphany also commemorates Jesus' baptism by John in the Jordan at the beginning of his public ministry, and his first miracle at the wedding at Cana. John concludes his account of the event by saying, "This was the first of the signs given by Jesus; it was given at Cana in Galilee.

He let his glory be seen, and his disciples believed in him" (Jn 2:11).

The word *epiphany* means a showing forth, a manifestation, a revelation. The visit of the Magi, Jesus' baptism by John and the miracle at Cana make manifest to the world, to Jew and Gentile alike, that the baby born in Bethlehem on Christmas night is truly the Messiah, the Savior of the world. It was not enough that he come to our world as one of us; his coming also had to be clearly revealed to us. Only then could we believe in and accept him as our Savior and the Lord of our life.

In the first part of this book we saw the very gradual evolution of the church's thinking concerning the world in which we live our lives. As the centuries passed, and as spirituality moved from desert to monastery to marketplace, a gradual epiphany of the Lord's presence in his and our world took place. He had come long ago to Mary and Joseph, and then to those who were his own. But as John says in the prologue to his gospel:

> He was in the world,
> that had its being through him,
> and the world did not know him.
> He came to his own domain
> and his own people did not accept him (Jn 1:10-11).

John's literal reference is to the Jewish people, but our reflections thus far make clear that his words also apply to us who belong to the church of Jesus. We too have been very slow to realize that he is in the world and that this world is now his own country.

Patiently and repeatedly he manifests himself to us, and ever so slowly we begin to see. In the church's life as much as in Jesus' own life, incarnation and epiphany are inseparably linked. The Lord takes flesh in our world and in us, but our humanity demands that this incarnation be made manifest, that it show itself visibly in our lives. We are not angels but human beings. Our deepest experiences must be visibly embodied in our actions. They must be enfleshed, and not be merely "in our heads." Incarnation must be completed by epiphany, inner faith experience by good works, knowing by doing.

In the first epistle of John, we read:

> We can be sure that we know God
> only by keeping his commandments. . . .
> Anyone who claims to be in the light
> but hates his brother is still in the dark
> (1 Jn 2:3,9).

To cite just one more famous and blunt verse from the same epistle:

> Anyone who says, "I love God,"
> and hates his brother,
> is a liar,
> since the man who does not love the brother
> that he can see
> cannot love God, whom he has never seen.
> So this is the commandment that he has given us,
> that anyone who loves God must also love his brother (1 Jn 4:20-21).

This central New Testament theme tells us that we can know God primarily through his creation, and that we cannot know and love God if we do not know and love the world around us.

With regard to lay spirituality, it is not enough that we know and affirm that the laity are called to the fullness of Christian life and holiness; we must act on that call. In the second part of the book, I would like to reflect with you on the "doing" which must incarnate our knowing.

What Holiness Really Means

In chapter 5 of *Lumen Gentium*, the Second Vatican Council treats of the universal call of every Christian to holiness. It relates the life and activity of those who belong to Christ to their ultimate goal. All that we have and are, all our rights and duties as disciples of Christ in the world today, are ordered to one ultimate end: holiness. "Before the world was made, he chose us, chose us in Christ, to be holy and spotless, and to live through love in his presence" (Eph 1:4).

The scriptural call to holiness is clear enough, but the challenge faced by Vatican II was to spell out its meaning in a way consistent with her whole vision of the church, specifically of the central place of the laity in that church. The council begins by stressing that the church herself is holy because Christ her Lord is holy:

> He united her to Himself as His own body, and crowned her with the gift of the Holy Spirit, for God's glory. Therefore in the Church, everyone belonging to the hierarchy, or being cared for by it, is called to holiness, according to the saying of the Apostle: For this is the will of God, your sanctification (1 Thes 4:3; cf. Eph 1:4) (No. 39).

To be called holy would make most of us uncomfortable since it seems to connote an otherworldliness, an alienation from the ordinary concerns and failings of normal human beings. If we think someone else is perceived as holy we may be ill at ease in their presence, as if holy people are plastic saints or are swallowed up in some ecstatic state unknown to us ordinary mortals. The problem here is with the word *holy* as people ordinarily use it. For a long time instead of seeking holiness, I have preferred desiring to be a truly *loving* person—in love with God and in love with his people. I encourage my directees to desire this as well. It seems more real, and more attainable, than the elusive goal of holiness. And it involves much less danger of a self-centered and ultimately pride-inducing pursuit of perfection.

The council does speak of holiness and of our need

to "be perfect, just as your heavenly Father is perfect" (Mt 5:48). But it makes clear that this perfection is Jesus' work and not ours: "He Himself stands as the Author and Finisher of this holiness of life" (No. 40). And, even more important, it insists that holiness means above all else "the fullness of Christian life and the perfection of charity." The holy person is the truly loving person, the one who shares Jesus' own passion for the Father and for the doing of his will. Since charity is patient and kind, long-suffering and well-mannered (see 1 Cor 13:4-7), the loving person is a joyful companion, not someone who makes us feel guilty and uneasy.

Of course, not everyone will like the loving person, just as not everyone liked Jesus Christ despite his gracious and caring manner. Jesus was perfectly holy, so the resentment of others was not due to him but rather to their jealousy and insecurity. He made some people uncomfortable because his goodness held up a mirror to reveal their own hypocrisy. None of us can be that blameless in our own way of acting and loving, since we are not as totally committed to God as Jesus. At times it will be our own fault, or because of our own human limitations, that others dislike us. But the more we grow in grace, the more like him in his gentle and yet courageous attitude we will be, and that is true holiness.

In the lengthy and beautiful paragraph 41, Vatican II proceeds to show how this authentic ideal of holiness applies to every vocation within the church: bishops, priests, deacons, those involved in the lay apostolate, married couples and parents, widows and single persons, laborers, the sick and the persecuted. In each case, the way to holiness is that proper to one's particular vocation. For example, married people become holy "by faithful love, sustaining one another in grace throughout the entire length of their lives." And parents "should imbue their children, lovingly welcomed from God, with Christian truths and evangelical virtues." This is the way to holiness, to the perfection of charity in the lay, married life.

No one would claim that holiness is easy. Whether one is a cloistered nun, a parish priest, a married or single lay person, to become truly loving is a lifetime struggle. But it *is* possible. And it is down-to-earth. The grace of God can effect the perfection of charity in any Christian in any state of life, provided only he or she is willing to allow the Lord the freedom to accomplish his wonders.

The Concrete Signs of True Life in Christ

Those who insist that our sanctification is completely God's work, and in no way depends on our own efforts, frequently appeal to Paul in defence of their position. It is true that, especially in Romans and Galatians, he insists that we are not justified by the works of the Law of Moses. He is reacting against his own pharisaical background with its stress on the meticulous observance of every minute detail of the Old Testament Law:

> We could have been justified by the law if the
> Law we were given had been capable of giving
> life, but it is not; scripture makes no exceptions
> when it says that sin is master everywhere. In
> this way the promise can only be given
> through faith in Jesus Christ and can only be
> given to those who have this faith (Gal 3:21-22).

Paul opposes the observance of the Old Testament Law to the free gift of faith in Christ Jesus. The Law reveals our sinfulness, since even the best of us cannot, by his or her own efforts, observe its prescriptions. By contrast, faith in Christ "justifies" those who cannot achieve their own righteousness before God. However, it is a mistake to conclude from this that Paul sees our own efforts to live a good life as unimportant. He himself raises the objection in his letter to the Romans:

Does it follow that we should remain in sin so
as to let grace have greater scope? Of course
not. We are dead to sin, so how can we continue to live in it? . . . If in union with Christ
we have imitated his death, we shall also
imitate him in his resurrection. We must realize
that our former selves have been crucified with
him to destroy this sinful body and to free us
from the slavery of sin. When a man dies, of
course, he has finished with sin. . . . If I may
use human terms to help your natural weakness: as once you put your bodies at the
service of vice and immorality, so now you
must put them at the service of righteousness
for your sanctification (Rom 6:1-2,5-7,19).

Paul tries to walk a fine line between two extremes
here. On one side is the passivity of those who leave
everything to Christ. In the Philippines we have an often-
used saying which expresses perfectly this extreme: *Tayo
ay tao laman*, "we are only human." It can be used to
excuse every failure and act of negligence. Since we are
only human, what more can be expected of us? The other
extreme, more common to those raised in an Anglo-Saxon
culture like my own American background, is the Pelagian
stress on self-activity—perfection as *my own* project and
responsibility. A common saying for those on this extreme
would be: God helps those who help themselves.

According to Paul the gospel truth is somewhere in
the middle. The work of our sanctification is indeed 99
percent God's. But that other one percent, our response
to his gracious initiative, is crucial. In making concrete
what this entails, one of Paul's favorite metaphors is
clothing. For example, he says:

You are God's chosen race, his saints; he loves
you, and you should be clothed in sincere
compassion, in kindness and humility, gentleness and patience. Bear with one another;

forgive each other as soon as a quarrel begins.
The Lord has forgiven you; now you must do
the same. Over all these clothes, to keep them
together and complete them, put on love (Col
3:12-15).

There are two noteworthy points in this beautiful
passage. First, our good deeds are primarily those concerned with our acceptance of and concern for one another. And secondly, "The Lord has forgiven you; now
you must do the same." Because God has first loved us,
our acceptance of others is our act of thanksgiving to the
Lord for accepting us.

This same note of grateful response is also prominent
in another famous clothing passage from Paul's letter to
the Ephesians. Here he gives the clothing metaphor a
characteristically masculine military twist, based on his
conviction that our life is a warfare with the army of
Satan.

For it is not against human enemies that we
have to struggle, but against the Sovereignties
and the Powers who originate the darkness of
this world, the spiritual army of evil in the
heavens. That is why you must rely on God's
armor, or you will not be able to put up any
resistance when the worst happens, or have
enough resources to hold your ground. So
stand your ground, with *truth buckled round
your waist*, and *integrity for a breastplate*, wearing
for shoes on your feet *the eagerness to spread the
gospel of peace*, and always carrying the shield
of faith so that you can use it to put out the
burning arrows of the evil one. And then you
must accept *salvation from God to be your helmet*,
and receive the word of God from the Spirit to
use as a sword. Pray all the time, asking for
what you need, praying in the Spirit on every
possible occasion (Eph 6:12-18).

Truth, integrity, zeal to spread the gospel, faith and prayer—the concrete signs of our life in Christ differ in this passage. They provide a strong complement to the gentle list in Colossians (compassion, kindness, humility, patience, tolerance, forgiveness, love) so that the two lists together give us a comprehensive picture of true Christian holiness. One thing, however, is common to both passages: the stress on our receptivity, on the primacy of God's gracious gift to which our virtuous life is a grateful response. We must "accept salvation from God" as our helmet, and "receive the word of God from the Spirit" as our sword.

Faith, Hope and Love

In all we have said thus far about the concrete signs of true life in Christ, no distinction is made or implied between lay Christians and priests or religious. The gospel ideal is indeed challenging, but it is not presented as the ideal only of some elite class of Christians. It is for anyone who truly wishes to follow Jesus Christ. At the same time, the living of this ideal will clearly demand of any disciple a regimen of commitment and discipline. The specific application will vary depending on one's state of life, but the essential demands of discipleship will be the same.

The first and most basic of these demands is that we grow in the deepest and most interior virtues of Christian life: faith, hope and love. As Paul says in another "military" passage, "Let us put on faith and love for a breast-plate, and the hope of salvation for a helmet." In *The Ascent of Mount Carmel*, St. John of the Cross relates these three theological virtues to the three faculties of our human spirit: faith to the intellect; hope, the memory; love, the will. By faith we accept the truths of revelation. By hope, based on our memory of the goodness of God in our lives thus far, we trust confidently in his promises and his future fidelity. And by love we unite our wills to his in the accomplishment of his loving design for us. While we cannot sharply separate faith, hope and love in our lives, the distinction can help us to clarify the various aspects of authentic interior growth and holiness.

How do we grow in faith and hope and love? Of course, every good deed in our lives is a means to this growth. But I would like to suggest that two essential and fundamental means are personal prayer and the Holy Eucharist. Properly understood, both lead us to a deepening of faith, of hope, and of love. While it is true that the Catholic tradition, like John of the Cross, has stressed the intellectual content of faith, our faith is still in *Someone*. We say in the Creed: "I believe in one God and in His Son, Jesus Christ." We believe *in* him, and not merely *that* he exists. Similarly, as Gabriel Marcel has made beautifully clear, we hope in Someone and not merely *for* some*thing*. We *expect* things to happen, but we *hope* in the one who makes them happen. Our expectations can get in the way of our hope: The more specific expectations I have on my checklist (I expect you to think of my needs . . . to take care of me . . . to do your duty), the less I hope in you. If I do trust you, hope in you as a person, then I can set aside my checklist confident that you will be true and loving whether or not my expectations are met.

It takes a long time to come to know a person well enough to trust her or him completely. And I suppose no mere human being can ever be totally true and trustworthy, although if we are fortunate there are some great loves in our lives that come close to the ideal. The marvelous thing about our God is that he is totally worthy of our trust. Even with him, however, we can only come to total trust as the fruit of long years of personal experience of him. And this personal experience is precisely what a good prayer life is all about.

I have written at length elsewhere about the dynamics of growth in personal prayer (*Opening to God* and *When the Well Runs Dry,* Ave Maria Press, 1977 and 1979). Moreover, there are numerous fine discussions, classic and contemporary, of the topic—many of which I referred to in those two books. For the present, I would merely like to underline the point that prayer is precisely the way we come to and sustain our "personal encounter with God in love" (*Opening to God,* chapter 1). Prayers can be the enemy of genuine prayer. That is, our talking—petitions, apologies, even acts of thanksgiving—good as it is, can get in the way of our truly listening to God. We cannot get to know someone if we talk all the time. We must listen, observe, be with, waste time with him or her. It is the same with the Lord.

For us Catholics our sacramental life, and especially our reception of the Holy Eucharist, is a privileged means of listening prayer. I have occasionally wondered what it would be like to be a Protestant rather than a Catholic. There are some very attractive features of the Protestant tradition, especially its deep knowledge and love of scripture and its pioneering stress on the laity as the heart and soul of the church. But what I would miss most if I were a Protestant is the whole sacramental life of the church, especially the Holy Eucharist. The intimate and bodily encounter with the Lord which the Eucharist effects must be one of the greatest gifts he could give to us human beings. We would be infinitely impoverished without it.

And yet, how many of us Catholics really appreciate the treasure we have? How many priests and religious, even, really experience the growth in faith and hope and love which should be the fruit of frequent or daily reception of the Eucharist? The reason why they are relatively few is, I think, because the Eucharist is not often seen as part of a wider life of personal prayer. As with our human friendships, times of celebration and moments of intimacy

are only as real and deep as the whole ongoing relationship which they celebrate and focus.

Spiritual life, too, whether lay or religious, is subject
to the laws of growth in intimacy. The time for formal
listening prayer need not be long—in my experience about
30 minutes a day is ideal and sufficient—but it is essential
to solid lay spirituality. At the beginning this will involve
searching the scriptures, not primarily for moralistic
guidelines for living but to get to know the God and
Father of Jesus Christ. Who is this Lord whom we are
drawn to love? What would it mean to live my life in
intimacy with him? What are his values and how do they
resonate with, or conflict with, my own? You and I cannot
observe Jesus as the disciples did. We cannot walk the
roads of Galilee and Samaria with him, hear him speak,
see his miracles. At least we cannot do these things
directly. But we can share vicariously the experience of the
disciples. This, in fact, is why the gospels were written,
so that we who did not know the Lord in the flesh 2,000
years ago may come to know and love and trust him, and
his Father, through the reminiscences of his first friends.

Grounding Action in Prayer

One of the most striking features of a good prayer
life, such as we have been describing is that we come to
know not only the Lord but ourselves. When two people
are dating, they learn much about each other, and at least
as much about themselves. In learning that his girlfriend
loves the ballet and dislikes basketball, a man comes to
realize how attached to his basketball games he is. If he is
not comfortable with some of her good friends, she
realizes how costly it will be to let go of, or at least
weaken, those friendships in order to spend her life with
him. Of course, in any healthy relationship, they also
discover common interests and values which would draw
them to make the sacrifices necessary to share their lives.
For better or worse, the relationship focuses much more

clearly on who they are and what they really desire to make of their lives as individuals as well as together.

It is the same with God. As we come to know him better, as we discover in scripture what kind of a person Jesus Christ really is, we also come to know ourselves much better. We experience our own hearts quickening as he shares his values and dreams. But we also find that friendship with him involves demands which we are reluctant to accept. As with any love, we will have to die to something of ourselves—our selfishness, our privacy, our attachments—in order to live in love with him. This is the costly side of love, and explains why so few marriages ever realize their full promise. Most marriages are neither total failure nor total success. The spouses do love one another. But they set a limit to their generosity, to the extent to which they are willing to die to themselves in order to become "two in one flesh."

The greatest tragedy is when the spouses (one or both of them) are not able to recognize that they are setting limits to their love. Then they blame the failure or mediocrity of their marriage on someone or something else: on their spouse, on circumstances, on the human condition. They fail to grow in self-knowledge and so they never mature. And again, the same is true of our relationship to God. We can easily set limits to our intimacy with him because the cost of growing deeper is too great. We don't wish to be naked before him because we don't really want to know ourselves. Because of this danger Francis de Sales, with all the great masters of spirituality, insists upon the importance of the examination of conscience and sacramental confession in any genuine spiritual life. These are the great tools for achieving a healthy and liberating self-knowledge. Properly understood and used, they free us to stand naked before the Lord of Love.

The daily examination of conscience need take only five or ten minutes, perhaps before retiring at night. It is not a time for introspective self-blame and soul-scraping. Nor should it foster scrupulosity, if done properly. Rather it is a time to look back in peace over the events of the day, to see where the Lord has been revealing himself in persons and events and how we have responded to his self-revelation. It is an exercise, we might say, in sensitivity training. We know by faith that God is present in every situation. But very few of us, especially when we are beginners in the spiritual life, have the eyes to see his presence. We are caught up in the "noise" of the present moment and fail to hear the "still small voice" (1 Kgs 19:12) of the Lord. The examination of conscience, or consciousness examen as it is often called today, is an opportunity to come to quiet at the end of a busy day and to become sensitive to the Lord's meaning in all that has been happening.

Thus the examen is an exercise of faith: It is grounded in the faith-conviction that the Lord is working in our lives and that all that happens to us does have a divine meaning. Similarly, the sacrament of reconciliation, or confession, is an expression of our faith and trust in the healing love of the Lord. In recent times there has been a falling off in the frequency with which devout Catholics approach the sacrament of reconciliation. This is understandable, considering that past confessional practice had been too one-sided. It focused too exclusively on our sins and failings. But it is now time for us to return to the sacrament with a renewed and positive sense of its place in our lives. The fathers of the church often referred to penance or reconciliation as the "sacrament of peace." The phrase is beautifully apt, since the fruit of reconciliation properly experienced should always be peace, not anxiety or turmoil or scrupulosity. Our "God is not a God of disorder but of peace" (1 Cor 14:33).

In order that the sacrament of reconciliation be a true instrument of peace and spiritual growth, it should be

approached in the same spirit as the consciousness examen. It is important for one who wishes to grow in the
Lord to choose his or her confessor with some care. This
is especially true if the confessor is seen as a spiritual
director, not merely one who absolves me but one who
journeys with me in my growth in holiness. Since we are
human beings and not angels, it is important that the
spiritual director be one to whom I can relate comfortably.

I am often asked how to choose a director, and over
the years I have come to reply that there are four qualities
one should look for in the director: first, that he or she be
on the same wave length, someone I am comfortable
with; second, one who believes in what I am seeking (for
example, it would be foolish for a person seeking to grow
in prayer to choose a director who does not pray or does
not see the relevance of prayer to an active, lay life); third,
one who can be objective in interpreting for me the ways
in which the Lord is working in my life; fourth, ideally
though not necessarily, one who is a bit ahead of me on
the journey toward "Jerusalem," toward holiness.

While a less experienced director can direct someone
more advanced (the famous example is the newly ordained Baltazar Alvarez's fruitful direction of St. Teresa of
Avila), the process is much surer and easier if the director's advice is based on personal experience. A spiritual
director can be a man or woman, lay, ordained or religious. While a sacramental confessor in the present
Catholic dispensation must be an ordained male, and
while it is very helpful to be able to integrate confession
and spiritual direction, it is even more important to
choose a director, whether woman or man, who possesses
for me the first three qualities I mentioned above. They
imply a balance of loving concern and objectivity. The
director is a friend, sharing my dreams and hopes and
resonating to my feelings and fears. But he or she is a
special kind of friend, one who does not make my prob-

toe. Each is also part of a body. And in some mysterious
way which we Christians have barely begun to grasp after
2,000 years, we are called to holiness as a community. In
the beautiful words of the First Epistle of Peter we are "a
chosen race, a royal priesthood, a consecrated nation, a
people set apart to sing the praises of God" (1 Pt 2:9). In
the chapters to follow we will explore this communitarian
dimension of our call to holiness. It is, we have suggested, what distinguishes Vatican II from the earlier work
of Francis de Sales. It is also, to use a favorite expression
of Father John Courtney Murray, the "growing edge" of
our contemporary understanding of Christian spirituality.

♣ Chapter Six
Celibacy and Hierarchy in the Age of the Laity

Various Ways to One End

In my work as a spiritual director in a diocesan seminary, I have come to realize that the seminarians cannot hope to live celibacy fruitfully and happily unless they have a genuine appreciation of marriage and the lay life. To be celibate is to be wedded to the Lord, and one can scarcely understand or value such a supernatural state without a positive sense of marriage, the human metaphor that gives meaning to celibacy. One cannot see celibacy merely as an escape, a renunciation of human sexuality as something evil or "dirty." The celibate does renounce marriage, but not as something bad. Rather, he or she sees it as one of the most precious gifts of God to his human beings, and says to the Lord, "Because I love you so much, my God, I would like to offer to you something of supreme value to me. The value and the beauty of my gift is a measure of my love for you."

How do the seminarians come to that positive appreciation for marital intimacy? Usually by coming from happy homes, where their own parents are the best advertisement for the joys of married life. It is possible for a good religious vocation to come from an unhappy home situation. But it is much more difficult, and requires much healing love and much divine grace during the formation years. As we have said before, grace builds on nature.

And in my experience most successful religious vocations
do come from happy homes—not perfect marriages, since
no human relationship, even the best, is ever completely
idyllic, but basically happy and stable family environ-
ments. Celibacy is thus not an escape or a flight from
frustration and disappointment, but an affirmation that
the person drawn to a centering love of God is securely
grounded in human love.

As I now reflect on the topic of lay spirituality, it
strikes me that the converse of the above should also be
true. That is, if one is to live marriage fruitfully as a
Christian sacrament, she or he must have a positive
appreciation for the celibate vocation. This may be a more
surprising claim. But it is borne out, I believe, by a classic
essay of Rosemary Haughton, entitled "Marriage and
Virginity: Two Ways to One End." [1] She argues that the
two vocations, marriage and virginity (or celibacy), are
really complementary. Each needs the other to reveal the
fullness of life proclaimed by Jesus in the gospel. The goal
of both is full Christian maturity. But they are "two (distinct) ways to one (single) end." Each has its own
strengths and its own limitations. And both are processes
of growth toward a common goal. In the end they converge. Both are calls "to leave all things and follow
Christ."

In Chapter VII we will explore more fully Rosemary
Haughton's ideas in this important article. For the moment, though, I would like to quote just two sentences in
support of my claim that a good Christian marriage
requires a positive appreciation of the value of celibacy.
She says, "It is perhaps rash for someone who is married
to write about religious life. I do so because of my conviction . . . that Christian marriage makes no sense as Chris-

---

[1] Found in *The Gospel Where It Hits Us* (London: Geoffrey Chap-
man, 1968), pp. 1-13.

tian unless it looks beyond itself to the goal signified by the life of consecrated virginity." Unless the centering love of God, which is symbolized by virginity or celibacy, is recognized as the goal of every good marriage, the spouses will never realize the full meaning and promise of their marriage vows.

It is from this perspective that I would like to discuss celibacy and priestly hierarchy in the present chapter. As we said at the end of the last chapter, the lay Christian's spirituality must be both interior and exterior, involve both prayer and service, be lived in the marketplace as well as in the chapel. The exterior, service, marketplace dimension necessarily involves collaboration with religious and clergy. This fact alone would justify our speaking about religious life and the hierarchical priesthood. But Rosemary Haughton's insight takes us even deeper. More is at stake here than the question of apostolic collaboration between the religious and the laity. Neither vocation can discover its own goal and meaning without an appreciation of the other. Each *needs* to know and love the other to be itself.

With You I Am a Christian

We can begin our consideration of the celibate vocation in the Catholic church by discussing her priestly hierarchy. In the Introduction, I used the image of a pyramid to describe the change in attitude and action to which the Holy Spirit called us in the Second Vatican Council. If the church before Vatican II often saw herself as a pyramid of authority and holiness, then the council could be said to have inverted the pyramid. The church is the people of God—all of us, none of us any more Christian than any other. None of us is, simply by the fact of our state in life, any holier or any more called to holiness.

While it may have been neglected in the past, many of the saints and great spiritual writers have realized that the gospel demanded of them an "inverted pyramid" vision of the church. Perhaps the most famous of the testimonies to our universal call to holiness is that of the great St. Augustine. Converted and baptized in his 30s by St. Ambrose in the year 387, Augustine returned to his native Africa. There he was bishop of Hippo for 34 years until his death in 430 A.D. He was also, with St. Thomas Aquinas and Origen, one of the greatest theologians the church has produced. Of the three, he was the most literary and poetic, and consequently the most personalistic in his style of theologizing.

A beautiful example of the Augustinian approach pertains to our topic. Vatican II in *Lumen Gentium* (Chapter IV, No. 32) quoted from one of his sermons in confirmation of its vision of the laity, who have for their brothers in the faith both Christ Jesus himself and "those in the sacred ministry." Augustine had said, in addressing his people in Hippo: "What I am for you terrifies me; what I am with you consoles me. For you I am a bishop; but with you I am a Christian. The former is a duty; the latter a grace. The former is a danger; the latter, salvation."

Very few of us could express this truth as beautifully as Augustine did. But every priest and bishop must, if he really appreciates and is sincere about his vocation, share the feelings of Augustine. At least at times, sometimes more than others, he will be "terrified" by his priestly burden, precisely because he recognizes it as a "duty" and a "danger." Far from seeing it as a claim to privilege and ease, he will recognize that it is fundamentally a responsibility to the Lord and to God's people. And he will also recognize the danger of using for his own advantage the authority which the Lord has given him as an instrument of service.

Not infrequently, seminarians who are approaching ordination are overwhelmed by the immensity of the challenge which faces them. When they speak to me about it, I always tell them their fear is a very healthy sign. If they did not feel anxious—and the same would apply to a young couple on the eve of their marriage—I would really be concerned. I would question their maturity and their adult grasp of the seriousness of the step they were about to take. Augustine, too, was terrified, so they are in very good company.

Fortunately, though, this is only half of the story. St. Augustine was not only a bishop *for* his people; he was also a Christian *with* them. And it was his latter identity, which he calls a "grace" and "salvation," which consoled him in the face of his daunting responsibilities. Yves Congar, O.P., in *A Gospel Priesthood* (Herder and Herder, 1967, p. 93), quotes this passage of Augustine and then adds a favorite 17th-century saying of the spiritual director, Abbe Huvelin, "A priest, after finishing his functions at the altar or his ministrations of the sacraments, should, in some way or other resume his place among the laity." Huvelin explains this saying as follows:

> Hence a priest, for instance, who preached on the Gospel of the Sower should take his place in the congregation to listen, in his own turn, to the parable, and ask himself if he be not the soul on which the seed was wasted because it fell by the wayside. . . . After having heard confessions and given absolution, he should take his place on his knees among the laity and ask himself (with Judas at the Last Supper): Is it I, Lord?

Augustine and Huvelin and Congar are men of the "inverted pyramid" church. And so is the young priest who finds his ministry *for* his people a daunting challenge—provided only that he also realizes, and is consoled by the realization, that he is first a Christian *with* his people. He is their "wounded healer." Together he and they comprise the people of God.

The Wounded Healer

Our purpose in this book is to explore the lay vocation to holiness in the light of Vatican II. However, since
most of us have been raised in a pyramidal, "eggs-to-the-
Poor-Clares" model of the church, and since we seek in
this chapter a deeper appreciation of the complementarity
of the celibate and the lay vocations, let us dwell a bit
longer on the true role of the clergy in the church of Jesus
Christ. Specifically, let us ask why Augustine saw his call
to be a bishop as a "danger." Even if we accept his conviction that he is one with his people in the saving grace of
being a Christian, doesn't it sound strange to refer to his
elevation to the rank of bishop as "dangerous"? We might
be more inclined to call it an honor, a privilege, a call to
higher service, a confirmation of his priestly effectiveness.
But why a "danger"?

Another great figure from the early church, Gregory
the Great, can make clear for us what Augustine had in
mind. Gregory, who lived about 150 years after Augustine, was not only a bishop but one of the great popes of
history (590-604). He renounced a career in public service
to become a Benedictine monk shortly after the death of
Benedict himself. And he was called from the monastic
life to be the pope at one of the critical moments in the
early church's life.

During his papacy Gregory preached a homily on
Ezekiel which is used as the reading for his feast, Septem-
ber 3. The line in Ezekiel which he takes as his text is:
"Son of Man, I have made you a watchman for the house
of Israel." Let me quote part of his reflections on the
dangers of the watchman's calling,

> Note that a man whom the Lord sends forth as a
> preacher is called a watchman. A watchman always
> stands on a height so that he can see from afar what is

coming. Anyone appointed to be a watchman for the people must stand on a height for all his life to help them by his foresight.

The watchman's calling is a noble one, and yet Gregory immediately adds,

How hard it is for me to say this, for by these very words I denounce myself. I cannot preach with any competence and yet insofar as I do succeed, still I myself do not live my life according to my own preaching. . . . Indeed when I was in the monastery I could curb my idle tongue and usually be absorbed in my prayers. Since I assumed the burden of pastoral care, my mind can no longer be recollected; it is concerned with so many matters.

Gregory goes on to enumerate the concerns which now fill his mind as pope: the affairs of the church and of monasteries; the lives and acts of individuals; the concerns of the citizens of Rome since the pope was, and is, the bishop of Rome; "the invasions of roving bands of barbarians" at a time when the Roman empire was in its final stage of decay; all the ordinary administrative demands of his office. And he concludes, "With my mind divided and torn to pieces by so many problems, how can I meditate or preach wholeheartedly without neglecting the ministry of proclaiming the gospel?"

This is but a part of Gregory's very personal and touching reflection on the hazards of his calling as pope, but it may suffice to make clear why Augustine would see his bishopric as a "danger." St. Paul, of course, realized this danger long before. That is why he said: "I beat my body into subjection lest, having preached to others, I myself become a castaway" (1 Cor 9:27). And in our time Henri Nouwen has entitled his famous book on ministry *The Wounded Healer.* That is what the priest or apostle is: a wounded healer, in need of the very healing which he or she mediates to others.

In the light of all that we have said, the "danger" of which Augustine spoke should be clear enough. Today, however, we can also see this danger in a new light. The concerns of which Gregory spoke are, after all, not *essentially* different from the challenges which any lay person faces in trying to live a committed Christian life in the world. Gregory was nostalgic for the peace and freedom of the monastic life, and many of us have echoed his nostalgia. But he became a *saint* and came to be known to history as "the Great" precisely *in* and because of the world which seemed so frustrating to his noble desires. Perhaps God sees things differently—not only in the life of Gregory, but also in our busy, confused and often frustrating lives. Maybe what we consider an obstacle to holiness is really, in God's eyes, the "sandpaper" of our sanctification!

Religious Life and "Perfect Love"

What we have said about priesthood and hierarchy in the inverted pyramid church of Vatican II is necessarily very brief. The council devoted many pages to priestly formation and ministry—summoning the clergy to a real renewal of life and spirit in our day. For our purposes, however, what we have said may suffice to make clear that the priestly order in the church is called to a ministry of service to the laity. In the final section of this chapter we will consider the concrete and practical applications which the council draws from this vision of service and collaboration. First, though, it would be good to recall that not all celibates are members of the priestly hierarchy. In addition to the laity and the clergy, there are also religious in the church.

Some religious are also clergymen. For example, most Dominicans and Franciscans whom you will meet are priests. But these clerical congregations, as they are called, also have non-priest members or "brothers." And there are religious communities of men, like the Christian

Brothers and the Marist Brothers, whose members are all (or virtually all) brothers, i.e. non-priests. Moreover, all religious women in the Catholic church are at present non-priests.

All this can be very confusing to the average lay person. The basic reality, however, is simply enough stated: The church embraces *three* distinct ways of following the gospel teaching of Jesus. At times they may overlap (for example, I am both a priest and a religious), but in their "pure" forms we find lay persons, priests, and vowed religious.

What does it mean to be a "religious" in the church? Essentially it is to be committed to a celibate following of Jesus Christ, as a member of a community or congregation recognized by the church. While present legislation requires that most priests be unmarried, we all know of recent exceptions. For example, men who have been ministers in their own Protestant denominations have, upon conversion to Catholicism, been allowed to receive priestly ordination while continuing in the married state. Priesthood is essentially (as St. Augustine told us) a function, a role of service in the community, for which celibacy is considered helpful. But it is not an *essential* condition of priestly ministry that the priest be unmarried. The church's legislation on this matter could conceivably change. Indeed, it took several centuries for the early Roman church to decide that her clergy should be celibate. And the Eastern or Oriental Catholic churches have always allowed their clergy to marry.

By contrast, celibacy is at the very heart of the religious life. This is Rosemary Haughton's point of reference in contrasting marriage and virginity as "two ways to one end." The religious, by professing vows of celibacy, poverty and obedience, proclaims that God is "enough"—to use the beautiful phrase of David Knight in *Cloud by Day, Fire by Night*. He or she casts aside the treasure of marriage in order to proclaim to God and the world (and self!) that he or she can be whole, with the love of God alone at the center of his or her life. God can fulfill lives and they can become truly fruitful because of his strong and personal love.

Vatican II also discusses the religious life in *Lumen Gentium*, the basic document of the council on the church. Indeed, the bishops saw fit to add a separate document on *The Appropriate Renewal of the Religious Life*. This is its English title. In Latin its title is taken from the opening words, *Perfectae Caritatis* ("Of Perfect Charity"). The document begins:

> In its Constitution which begins, "The Light of the World" (*Lumen Gentium*), this sacred synod has already pointed out how the teaching and example of the Divine Master laid the foundation for a pursuit *of perfect charity* through the exercise of the evangelical counsels and how such a pursuit serves as a blazing emblem of the heavenly kingdom (No. 1).

So the evangelical counsels of celibacy, poverty and obedience are an expression of the religious's love for God and his people; they are the means to achieve that perfect love of which the council speaks. Moreover, the vowed life is lived in and for the church. It is not merely a question of private devotion. As the bishops stated in *Lumen Gentium*: "By the charity to which they lead, the evangelical counsels join their followers to the Church and her mystery in a special way. Since this is so, the spiritual life of these followers should be devoted to the whole Church" (No. 44).

This same commitment to service is stressed again in *Perfectae Caritatis* (Number 5 and Number 10), where some of the apostolic works (educating the young, caring for the sick) are explicitly mentioned. One reason for the vowed life of religious is to be free to serve the church—

free from commitments to family and a secular job in order to be free for those most in need in the church and the community. There is, however, another, more symbolic role which religious life plays in the church. The council fathers express it poetically in the introduction to *Perfectae Caritatis* when they speak of the vowed life as "a blazing emblem of the heavenly kingdom." By this is meant that the celibate life is a sign to the church and the world, a reminder and a promise that, while we do not have here a lasting city, the Lord has prepared an everlasting dwelling place for all of us.

It is often said that religious life is an "eschatological" sign, a sign of the end-time, of the goal and ultimate purpose of our human existence. As such, it is a direct denial of the popular call to "eat, drink and be merry, for tomorrow we die." By renouncing marriage and possessions, the religious proclaims that tomorrow is not the end nor death the goal. The real power of this symbolic proclamation was brought home to me by my sister-in-law many years ago. While struggling to raise six children, she would ride her bicycle several miles to attend Mass every morning. I once asked her if she resented the sisters who lived right beside the church. They could virtually roll out of bed and into church for Mass—and with no crying children to worry about. Did she envy them? Not at all, she replied; on the contrary, they (and the religious structure of their lives) gave her hope in her own demanding marketplace. They were a sign to her that there is more to life than changing diapers and paying bills. They held out to her a promise of better things to come.

Not all religious, of course, live fully and fruitfully the life they profess—just as not all married people live theirs as it should be lived. But the ideal is a beautiful one, and it is essential to the church that there are those who live it well. They proclaim that God is our "enough." They free themselves to serve and love those who have no one to love and serve them. And they stand as a "blazing emblem" of the goal and meaning of a daily life in which it is all too easy to lose sight of the forest because of the trees. In all these ways vowed religious are essential to the life and holiness of the church. They do not stand apart from the laity, the "people of God," but rather are a yeast which can leaven the whole Body of Christ.

Women in Ministry

As we have said, vowed religious can be either women or men. In the previous section, all that we have discovered of their place in the church applies to both. But since the question of the role of women in the ministerial life of the church is an especially live one today, it might be helpful to reflect further on it. In the Catholic church, priesthood has traditionally been reserved to men. At the same time, perhaps from 65 to 75 percent of the religious in the church today are women—even if we include all priests among the men. While this anomaly was not particularly troublesome in the past, recent development, including various women's rights and women's liberation movements around the world, have raised our consciousness. This has been true especially in the United States and Western Europe. But, surprisingly perhaps, the bishops of Vatican II recognized the universal challenge as early as the 1960s.

The question of women's rights and responsibilities has been seen as an important part of the larger question of the rights of "minorities" in the church and in the world. The council, too, spoke directly and with courage on the rights of third world countries, of the poor, of racial minorities, of the handicapped. When I looked for specific references to women, I found relatively few (about five). But those few are striking and significant. Most appear in the famous document entitled *The Church in the Modern World*, which was added to the council agenda at the request of several of the "progressive" bishops (including Cardinal Montini, later Pope Paul VI). These bishops felt that the council should issue a special document which would enter into dialogue with the modern world concerning the most pressing problems of the day. The resultant decree is probably the most pastoral and concrete statement ever issued by a church council.

Early in the text, the council enumerates "the broader desires of mankind" to which they wish to respond. Among these, we read: "Where they have not yet won it, women claim for themselves an equity with men before the law and in fact" (No. 9). And how does the council respond to this claim? They say somewhat later:

> True, all men are not alike from the point of view of varying physical power and the diversity of intellectual and moral resources. Nevertheless, with respect to the fundamental rights of the person, every type of discrimination, whether social or cultural, whether based on sex, race, color, social condition, language or religion, is to be overcome and eradicated as contrary to God's intent. For in truth it must still be regretted that fundamental personal rights are not yet being universally honored. Such is the case of a woman who is denied the right and freedom to choose a husband, to embrace a state of life, or to acquire an education or cultural benefits equal to those recognized for men (No. 29).

There are two other, briefer references to the rights of women in this same pastoral document. We read, "Children, especially the younger ones, need the care of their mother at home. This domestic role of hers must be safely preserved, though the legitimate social progress of women should not be neglected on that account" (No. 52). And a few pages later the council notes that: "Women are now employed in almost every area of life. It is appropriate that they should be able to assume their full proper role in accordance with their own nature. Everyone should acknowledge and favor the proper participation of women in cultural life" (No. 60). So it seems clear that Vatican II takes its stand solidly with the women of today who "claim for themselves an equity with men before the law and in fact." This is not to say that the council solved all the practical problems involved in the question of women's rights. Even in the church we still have a long way to go to full equality. But this should not blind us to the distance we have already travelled—not only from the Judaeo-Roman view of the status of women reflected in Paul's letters, but also from more recent male chauvinist attitudes.

Perhaps this evolution, past and future, is nowhere more striking than in the lives and ministry of women religious. In the recent past even the most apostolic of congregations lived what was in effect a semi-cloistered life. And their apostolates were generally narrowly restricted to teaching and hospital work. Today women are involved in virtually every area of apostolic endeavor, in social justice work, in retreat giving, and in parochial ministry. The change has been striking even in a more traditional culture like the Philippines where President Aquino, while campaigning for the presidency in 1986, still had to face the insulting criticism of her opponent— that a woman's proper place was in the bedroom and not in the president's office. The slur helped her much more than it hurt her in the campaign, despite the fact that not a few men (and, surprisingly, women) resonated in their hearts to ex-President Marcos' chauvinistic attitude. Whatever their traditionalist views, however, the majority of Filipinos could no longer accept such a narrow idea of the place of women in public life.

My point is this: I believe the emergence of women religious as an important apostolic and social force had done much to effect this change of attitude. And Cory Aquino's victory, and subsequent success and courage under fire, has in turn contributed greatly to the ongoing emergence of religious women. The process is indeed slow. But we are moving. And Father John Courtney Murray's remark about the 50-year time span required to realize fully the work of the Spirit in the council can give us hope and patience in this area too.

In chapter III of the *Decree on the Apostolate of the Laity*, the bishops say: "Since in our times women have an ever more active share in the whole life of society, it is very important that they participate more widely also in the various fields of the Church's apostolate" (No. 9). We have seen that women religious are indeed participating more widely in the church's apostolic life. And there is no doubt their participation will continue to expand and diversify in the years to come. But the council is not speaking here only of *religious* women. The call is to *all* women, and indeed, to all Christians. One of the greatest contributions women religious have made in recent times may well be to have opened the windows of the church to a wider and richer participation in her life by all their lay sisters and brothers.

The Rights and Duties of the Laity in the Church

When a young person asks the question, "Do I have a vocation?", he or she is invariably thinking of the priesthood or the religious life. Someone who "does not have a vocation" is thus relegated to the lay life. But we have discovered throughout this book that the lay life is itself a vocation, a call from God. The lay state is not just the *basurahan* (garbage can) of the church, but a high and noble calling. As we have seen, it is just as much a call to holiness as the religious life or the priesthood. This is one of the most important teachings of the Second Vatican Council.

In this chapter we have been considering the role of the clergy and of religious in the Vatican II church, particularly vis-à-vis the laity. Since Vatican II clearly affirms the dignity of the lay state and its important part in the priestly, prophetic and kingly mission of Jesus Christ, it is clear that clergy and laity are called to a co-responsible partnership in the work of the church, much like the equal partnership between man and woman in a good marriage. Each has a distinct role, but neither is subservient to the other. Since this has not been very well understood in the past, the council devotes a final paragraph (Number 37) of Chapter IV of *Lumen Gentium* to the rights and duties of the lay person in the church today.

The fundamental right of the laity vis-à-vis their priests is

> to receive in abundance from their sacred pastors the
> spiritual goods of the Church, especially the assistance
> of the Word of God and the sacraments. Every
> layperson should openly reveal to them his needs and
> desires with that freedom which befits a son of God
> and a brother in Christ (No. 37).

This is a delicate area since none of us enjoys criticism, and many of us find it hard to distinguish between honest suggestions and negative criticism. It may thus be necessary for the layperson to find diplomatic ways to present his or her suggestions. But the principle is clear: We are fed at the "two tables" of the Word of God and the Eucharist, as the fathers of the church beautifully describe the two parts of our Mass, and everyone has the right to sufficient and nourishing food.

The council fathers also mention that a layperson, because of his or her professional competence, may be "permitted and sometimes even obliged to express his opinion on things which concern the good of the Church." While this should always be done "in truth, in courage and in prudence, with reverence and charity toward those who by reason of their sacred office represent the person of Christ," still it should not be considered disloyal for a competent layperson to speak out on what concerns the good of the church. The council is here striving for that delicate balance which is participative obedience. Neither slavish docility nor self-willed independence is healthy for any mature community.

Vatican II also stresses the duty of the laity to pray for their pastors, who will one day have to render an account of their stewardship. At the same time, pastors are enjoined to

> recognize and promote the dignity as well as the responsibility of the laity in the Church. Let them willingly make use of their prudent advice. Let them confidently assign duties to them in the service of the Church, allowing them freedom and room for action. Further, let them encourage the laity so that they may undertake tasks on their own initiative (No. 37).

This is a high ideal of co-responsibility. It presupposes that we have mature pastors and mature lay people. And even then, because of diversities of temperament and background, I suppose we can never realize it perfectly in this life. But ideals are important even if we never fully live up to them. If we know what we *should* be, at least we have a direction, a goal for our growth.

The council fathers see many benefits resulting from this ideal situation of co-responsibility or, as they call it, "familiar dialogue." For the laity it will mean "a strengthened sense of personal responsibility, a renewed enthusiasm, a more ready application of their talents to the projects of their pastors." And the pastors in turn, "aided by the experience of the laity, can more clearly and more suitably come to decisions regarding spiritual and temporal matters" (No. 37).

In the end, of course, the goal is a more effective fulfillment of the mission of Christ in proclaiming the gospel to the world. That is the reason for the church's existence. And while the ideal may never be perfectly realizable, I do believe we have grown much in co-responsibility since the council ended more than 20 years ago.

Our lay people are more involved, our parishes are more alive, and many of our priests have been strengthened and revitalized by the partnership of the laity in their ministry. The journey is a long one, but we do seem to be travelling in the right direction!

♣ Chapter Seven

Marriage and the Single Life in the Age of the Laity

The Family as Church

President Cory Aquino of the Philippines has been quoted, in several interviews, as saying that she finds her role as mother and grandmother more fulfilling than her role as president. Given the extraordinary situation which she inherited upon becoming the Philippines' president, this is perhaps not very surprising. I well recall a conversation with a friend and directee who was prominent in the events leading up to the Philippine revolution. He said that his friends felt it would be unwise for any of them to seek to replace President Marcos. As one priest-adviser put it: "If you wish to be the *second* successor of Marcos, that is fine. But not the first. Whoever replaces him is sure to face disaster and chaos." Indeed, it is a measure of Cory Aquino's achievement that we have not had disaster and chaos. We have, however, lived on the very edge for much of this first year of freedom. As I say, it is not really surprising that Mrs. Aquino has been more fulfilled as grandmother than as president.

And yet I believe she meant her statement in a deeper sense. From all that I know and read of her, I think she would have said the same thing even if she had become president in normal and prosperous times. Her family is really the center of her life and the heart of her vocation. In fact, it seems that what her accession to the presidency has meant to her is that the whole Philippines and all Filipinos have become her extended family. She feels for them a responsibility and love analogous to her feelings for Ninoy Aquino and their children. Of course, Ninoy is dead, the children are raised and grandmothers have the happy prerogative of not worrying about the details of raising their grandchildren. No wonder the home situation seems more fulfilling than her national role. Perhaps 10 or 15 years from now she will *feel* the fulfillment of her years as president.

I was reminded of Cory Aquino's statement as I reflected on the beautiful vision of the family and of marriage proposed to us by Vatican II. While there are occasional references to family life and marriage in several documents, the principal statement is chapter I of part II of the pastoral decree on *The Church in the Modern World* (*Gaudium et Spes*). In this decree the council "yearns to explain to everyone how it conceives of the presence and activity of the Church in the world of today. Therefore, the Council focuses its attention on the world of men and women, the whole human family along with the sum of those realities in the midst of which that family lives" (No. 2). The first of the two parts of this document establishes the basic philosophical and theological principles concerning human nature, society, the value and the limits of human science and technology, and finally, in chapter IV, "The Church in the Modern World."

This part of the decree is more abstract and philosophical. In fact, when I guided a group of lay people in studying *The Church in the Modern World*, they found part I rather hard going. But it is important, since it clarifies the principles which must guide the council fathers and the church of succeeding years in their dialogue with the world of the late-20th century. In essence these principles are: that humanity, as created by God, is fundamentally good, but weakened by the pervasive effects of sin; that

man and woman are essentially social beings (not rugged
individualists), and yet society exists for the good of the
person and not vice-versa; that science and technology are
true and essential human goods, enjoying genuine autonomy within their own proper sphere of competence; and
finally, that the church's role is to accept all that is hu-
manly good and, by viewing it discerningly in the light of
divine revelation, to integrate it into a comprehensive
vision and order it to humanity's ultimate end.

The council thus tries to strike a balance, find a solid
middle ground, between religious fundamentalism and
naturalistic humanism. Unlike the fundamentalists, it
does not wish to turn its back on the modern world by
setting religion in opposition to the secular sphere. At the
same time, it rejects the naturalism of those like John
Dewey a generation ago who would see science as the
new "religion" of contemporary man, rejecting religion
and faith as a kind of primitive and now outdated answer
to the questions of science. Its own vision of the mutual
interdependence, and yet relative autonomy, of the secular
and the sacred, is implicit in our whole discussion of the
call of the lay person to sanctify, and to be sanctified
within, the secular world.

A concrete experience may help to clarify this important point for the average reader. Many years ago my
parents had a good friend and neighbor who was a
leading obstetrician in Rochester. When I was home, we
enjoyed sitting in the back yard in summer and talking
shop. He was a devout Catholic, who lived his faith in his
work. One day we were talking about the moral and
medical aspects of birth control, when he said to me,
"What makes me angry is when a woman comes to me
and says, 'Father X said I can use the birth-control pill.' I
always want to reply to her, 'Then you go and tell Father
X to give you a prescription!' " His point was not whether
birth control by means of the pill was right or wrong.

Rather, what he meant was that Father X could pronounce on the *moral* aspects of using the pill, but that the medical, scientific aspects were beyond his competence. Moreover, to make a sound moral judgment one must know the medical, scientific *facts*. How does the pill work? How does it control conception—and what are its side effects? Later in this chapter we will see what the council had to say about this important problem for marital and family life. The point here is that the church must depend on the medical ("secular") world for answers to these *scientific* questions. But once she knows the facts, she has the responsibility to make a judgment on the *morality* of the use of the pill. She does not decide in a vacuum. The sacred and the secular are interdependent in determining the total good of human beings, and each has a legitimate autonomy in its own proper sphere.

In part II of *The Church in the Modern World*, the council seeks to apply the general principles of part I to the most important areas of modern life. Chapter I, which is of special interest to us in this chapter, treats of marriage and family life. Then there are chapters on culture, socioeconomic life, politics, and a final chapter on fostering peace, in which the urgent questions of nuclear warfare and the United Nations are tackled. Basic to the discussion of marriage and the family is the biblical vision of the marital union of man and woman as a sacrament (a concrete, visible sign) of the union of Jesus Christ with his church. Vatican II refers several times to Paul's famous passage on marriage in Ephesians (5:21-33). While today we would have to interpret his culturally conditioned vision of woman as "subject" to man in the light of the council's clear statements on the fundamental equality of men and women, the central point of the passage is that the love between wife and husband mirrors the love of Christ for his church. The church is the spouse of Jesus Christ. "Husbands should love their wives just as Christ loved the Church and sacrificed Himself for her to make her holy."

The family, we can say, is the nuclear church, the core community in which the saving love of Christ is incarnated in our world. All the other areas of human concern—culture, economics, politics—which the council discusses ultimately depend on the well-being of the family. For this reason, Cory Aquino's statement about her own greatest fulfillment makes eminently good sense. And for this reason, too, we can appreciate Vatican II's insistence that the lay vocation is a true Christian vocation, and that the heart of this lay vocation is found precisely in marriage and the raising of a family.

Marriage as a Noble Way to Our Christian End

The section of *The Church in the Modern World* to which we have been referring (part II, chapter I) is noteworthy for several reasons. It is a clear reaffirmation of the traditional Christian teaching on the permanence of the marriage commitment, the importance of proper preparation for marriage, and the dignity and value of the married state. More interestingly, this chapter contains certain emphases which are new in conciliar teaching—emphases which reflect the council's desire to enter into dialogue with the contemporary world and to take seriously the best insights of modern thought. One of these new emphases we have already noted: the vision of the marital relationship as an equal partnership between man and woman. Each brings distinctive gifts to their union, and each depends on the other in certain ways. But they work together and decide together in planning to have and raise their children. Theirs is not a master-slave but a friend-friend relationship.

Another new emphasis in the chapter is very much related to this partnership. In the not so distant past it was customary to describe the primary end or purpose of

marriage as the procreation of children. A secondary end
was the "remedy of concupiscence," a negative phrase
which sounds strange today and which echoes Paul's
advice to the unmarried that "if they cannot control the
sexual urges, they should get married, since it is better to
be married than to be tortured [by passion]" (1 Cor 7:9).
Vatican II "corrected" this traditional teaching on the ends
of marriage in two important ways: It insisted that the
first end or purpose is not merely procreation, but rather
the procreation *and education* of children, and it expressed
the second but no longer secondary purpose positively, as
the fostering of mutual love.

In the modern world, with which the council wishes
to enter into fraternal dialogue, it is no longer true that
"the more the merrier" is a good norm for having children. In an earlier agrarian society to have many children
was an asset. They provided old age insurance for the
parents, did not have to be educated beyond the elementary level, if at all, and were a ready source of extra hands
on the farm. Moreover, if a couple had ten children, they
would consider themselves fortunate if four or five sur-
vived to adulthood. Today, however, all this has changed
in most parts of the world. Even in developing countries
the problem is not so much a soaring birth rate as a
declining death rate. And as society has urbanized,
having a large number of children has become more a
liability than an asset. They do need to be fed and educated, and they can no longer help on the farm in an
urban environment. Aware of all these momentous social
changes, the council states that "marriage and conjugal
love are by their nature ordained toward the begetting and
educating of children" (No. 50). In the next section we will
consider the conclusions which Vatican II draws from this
concerning the important questions of family planning
and birth control.

The other important development in church teaching

concerns what has traditionally been considered the secondary and thus subordinate end of marriage. The council in no way wishes to play down the importance of children in a true Christian marriage. At the same time, they recognize that human sexuality is not merely an animal act, tolerated with distaste because it is necessary for procreation. In a beautiful paragraph entitled "Conjugal Love" the fathers of the council affirm clearly that: "The biblical Word of God several times urges . . . the married to nourish and develop their wedlock by pure conjugal love and undivided affection" (No. 49). In a footnote to this sentence, several biblical passages are cited: Genesis 2:22-24; Proverbs 5:15-20, 31:10-31; Tobias 8:4-8; Canticle of Canticles 1:2-3, 1:16, 4:16, 5:1, 7:8-14; 1 Corinthians 7:3-6 and Ephesians 5:25-33. And the decree goes on to say: "Many men and women of our own age also highly regard true love between husband and wife, as it manifests itself in a variety of ways depending upon the worthy customs of various peoples and times" (No. 49).

In making its own this biblical and contemporary esteem for marriage, the council says:

> This love is an eminently human one since it is directed from one person to another. . . . It involves the good of the whole person. Therefore it can enrich the expressions of body and mind with a unique dignity, ennobling these expressions as special ingredients and signs of the friendship distinctive of marriage (No. 49).

The language is somewhat technical and abstract, but the essential point is clear. Marital love, including the sexual act of intercourse, is a truly human expression of friendship. As such it is good and holy, perhaps the deepest type of friendship possible between human beings.

> Such love, merging the human with the divine, leads the spouses to a free and mutual gift of themselves, a

gift proving itself by gentle affection and by deed. . . .
Therefore it far excels mere erotic inclination which,
selfishly pursued, soon enough fades wretchedly away
(No. 49).

The vision of sexuality here presented is far removed
from the old "remedy of concupiscence" language. And
lest anyone misinterpret their intent—the delicacy and
abstractness of the language could leave the impression
that some sort of "spiritual" friendship between spouses,
a sort of platonic friendship, is at issue here—the bishops
go on to say:

This love is uniquely expressed and perfected through
the marital act (intercourse). The actions within
marriage by which the couple are united intimately
and *chastely* are noble and worthy ones. Expressed in a
manner which is truly human, these actions signify
and promote that *mutual self-giving* by which spouses
enrich each other (No. 49).

I underlined two phrases in the quotation which merit
further comment: "chastely" and "mutual self-giving."

We may not be accustomed to think of chastity in
connection with marriage and intercourse, because we
often identify chastity with abstinence from immoral acts
and "dirty" thoughts. But chastity is a positive virtue, an
ordering of our loves according to their proper nature. In
marital friendship this means, as the council goes on to
say, remaining "steadfastly true in body and in mind, in
bright days and in dark. It will never be profaned by
adultery or divorce. Firmly established by the Lord, the
unity of marriage will radiate from the equal personal
dignity of wife and husband, a dignity acknowledged by
mutual and total love" (No. 49). And the council indicates
what is perhaps the most notable expression of marital
chastity when they say that "the couple will painstakingly
cultivate and pray for constancy of love, largeheartedness,
and the spirit of sacrifice" (No. 49).

The second phrase I underlined above is "mutual self-giving." This brings us back to the second end or purpose of marriage, and specifically of the marital act. To live faithfully, chastely and loyally in marriage for a whole lifetime is indeed very challenging. As the council says, it "demands notable virtue." And it is here that we can see the positive value of marital intimacy most clearly. As the Council said a bit earlier in discussing this second purpose of marriage,

> a man and a woman, who by the marriage covenant of conjugal love "are no longer two, but one flesh" (Matthew 19:6), render mutual help and service to each other through an intimate union of their persons and of their actions. Through this union they experience the meaning of their oneness, and attain to it with growing perfection day by day (No. 48).

Thus the expressions of marital intimacy, especially the act of intercourse, are far from being a mere concession to human weakness, a "remedy for concupiscence." They strengthen the couple to bear patiently with the difficulties and challenges inevitable in living so closely together. They unite them to face the daunting challenges involved in bearing and raising children. Intercourse is a powerful physical, embodied, truly human expression of the total gift of self, each to the other. No doubt this is the reason why the council, in a departure from past practice and exhortation, does not even recommend abstinence as a regular means of birth control. Occasional abstinence from intercourse, for example for reasons of health, will always have a place in marital self-giving. But long-term abstention from intercourse could deprive the couple of the support and strengthening love of one another at the very times when they most need it. Far from being virtuous, such abstinence could threaten the very commitment the married couple have made to save their souls together.

Children: Given in Trust for a Time

From all that we have just said, we can see clearly
the close connection between the two ends or purposes of
marriage. Even if the first end, the procreation and education of children, is impossible to realize in a particular
childless marriage, the second end is still realizable and
such a marriage can thereby be rich in Christian meaning.
But normally the two ends are to be achieved together.
The deepening of mutual love and generosity which
marital intimacy accomplishes gives the couple the joy
and strength and hope to have and raise their children in
a godly, Christian environment. At the same time the
children are the fruit, the concrete incarnation of their
union in love. To use a theme from Part I, the children are
the "epiphany" of their intimacy—the visible witness to
the love of Christ incarnate in their lives. And the children
also play a role in the sanctification of their parents. As
The Church in the Modern World puts it:

> As living members of the family, children contribute in
> their own way to making their parents holy. For they
> will respond to the kindness of their parents with
> sentiments of gratitude, with love and trust. They will
> stand by them as children should when hardships
> overtake their parents and old age brings loneliness
> (No. 48).

Of course, not all is sweetness and light. We are
sanctified by suffering and disappointment as much as by
success and joy. It is because the council is quite aware of
this that it acknowledges the importance of family planning in a good Christian marriage. We referred earlier to
the social and demographic changes which have led to a
rethinking of the church's teaching on procreation. The
gospel ideal remains constant and normative, but it must
be applied to the urbanized, industrialized world in which
more and more Christians live. Thus the council stresses
that couples must enter into marriage with a clear sense

of their responsibility for the procreation *and education* of whatever children they may have. This widened horizon has implications in two important areas: the decision concerning the number of children they should have, and the education they should give to the children actually born. The council addresses both questions.

Many people, including Catholics, seem to believe that the church is simply opposed to family planning or birth control. Fortunately or unfortunately, the truth is more complicated than that would suggest. To begin with, family planning and birth control refer to different, though related, realities. Family planning concerns the end, the goal, the plan. It has to do with the *decision* which the couple makes concerning the number of children they can best have *and raise* to the glory of God. Thus we could say that family planning is "in the head." It is, as the name suggests, a question of planning. By contrast, birth control refers to the means which may be used licitly in carrying out this plan. Among the possible means today are rhythm, abstinence, contraceptive pills, the diaphragm, the condom, withdrawal, and the "coil" or IUD. The moral question here is which of these means are acceptable for a committed Catholic to use.

So we have two questions concerning Christian procreation: family planning and birth control. As we shall see shortly, Vatican II had relatively little to say concerning birth control. But their teaching on family planning is clear and decisive. It is not only the right but the obligation of a devout couple to plan their family. We are human beings, and marital intercourse is a truly human act. We do not, and should not, merely procreate like rabbits and leave the result to fate or God. The council's discussion of this question is found in Number 50 of *The Church in the Modern World*. They stress that "children are really the supreme gift of marriage and contribute very substantially to the welfare of their parents." Moreover, they esteem highly those married Christians "who with wise and common deliberation, and with a gallant heart, undertake to bring up suitably even a relatively large family." Be sure to note, though, two important phrases, "with wise and common deliberation," and "to bring up suitably." It is not *always* better to have a large family. Circumstances must be evaluated wisely, and the couple must come to a *common* decision concerning family size.

In doing so, they should be stouthearted and faith-filled. To quote the relevant paragraph of Vatican II's teaching:

> Parents should regard as their proper mission the task of transmitting human life and educating those to whom it has been transmitted. They should realize that they are thereby cooperators with the love of God the Creator, and are, so to speak, the interpreters of that love. . . . With docile reverence towards God, they will come to the right decision by common counsel and effort (No. 50).

How do they make the decision? The council fathers next enumerate the factors to be considered.

> They will thoughtfully take into account both their own welfare and that of their children, those already born and those which may be foreseen. They will take into account both the spiritual and the material conditions of the times as well as of their own state in life. Finally, they will consider the best interests of the family, of civil society, and of the Church herself (No. 50).

Thus relevant factors in planning family size would be such as the health of the parents, the special needs of handicapped children already born, the present and foreseeable economic situation of the family, the present state of society, and so forth.

The council then makes the significant assertion that "the parents themselves should ultimately make this judgment in the sight of God." They must decide; it is *their* responsibility. Of course, as the decree hastens to add, "They cannot proceed arbitrarily. They must always be governed according to a conscience dutifully conformed to the divine law itself, and should be submissive to the Church's teaching" (No. 50). The divine law and the church's teaching, as St. Thomas Aquinas tells us, give us the general principles to guide our decisions. But these principles have to be applied to concrete, specific situations. This is the meaning of discernment in the Christian life, and the ones who make this discernment are the couple, for they have the grace of the sacrament of matrimony and they must live the decision made in faith and love.

This brings us to the question of birth control, the means to be used to realize the couple's decision concerning family size. The council, in Number 51, clearly and explicitly rejects abortion as an "unspeakable crime." And, more surprisingly, they also do not favor abstinence from intercourse as a means to limit family size, at least abstinence as a regular and sustained practice. As the decree says, "where the intimacy of married life is broken off, it is not rare for its faithfulness to be imperiled and its quality of fruitfulness ruined. For then the upbringing of the children and the courage to accept new ones are both endangered" (No. 51).

Apart from abortion and abstinence, however, Vatican II does not discuss any of the other possible means of birth control. The questions involved were much debated at that time, even in the council sessions, as was well known at the time. Since Pope Paul VI had established a commission in 1964 to study the whole question, the council contented itself with general statements of principle. Any means used must accord with the proper nature of human sexuality, respect human dignity, and be consistent with "the teaching authority of the Church in its unfolding of the divine law" (No. 51). About three years later Paul VI issued his famous decree (*Humanae Vitae*) stating that the only clearly acceptable means of birth control is rhythm or "natural family planning." While discussion continues even until now—and probably will continue for some time, since the medical aspects of the question are still far from clearly settled—we can say that rhythm or the variations of it which have evolved over the last 20 years should be a Christian couple's preferred means wherever possible.

The problem comes where the devout couple is convinced that their family should be limited, and yet rhythm (for reasons medical, psychological or even intellectual) does not seem possible. In that case, the couple should seek further advice from a good and informed priest or, if none is available, from a sister or lay person with the proper background in moral theology and counselling. Some of the means mentioned, particularly withdrawal and the IUD (which seems to be abortive), I would find clearly unacceptable. As for the others, we can hope that the medical and moral situation will become much clearer in the years ahead. In the meantime, we can scarcely do better than to imitate the great pastoral heart of Pope Paul VI who, in *Humanae Vitae*, urged his bishops and priests to be both firm in proclaiming sound doctrine *and* compassionate toward the real, sometimes agonized human beings who try to live this doctrine. Our hearts should go out to them in their dilemma: If they did not love the Lord, they would not be suffering! And, as St. Teresa said so beautifully, in the end we will be judged by love.

Before concluding this lengthy section, let us say a word concerning the other conciliar theme here, the education of the children whom a couple brings into the world. In *The Church in the Modern World* we are reminded that the parents bear the primary responsibility for the education, especially the religious education, of their children. They teach them by word and, even more, by the example of a good Christian life. And their primary responsibility includes sex education. "Especially in the heart of their own families, young people should be suitably and seasonably instructed about the duty, dignity and expression of married love" (No. 49). With regard to general education, the council states that "children be so educated that as adults they can, with a mature sense of responsibility, follow their vocation, including a religious one, and choose their state of life. If they marry, they can thereby establish their family in favorable moral, social and economic conditions" (No. 49).

The council also speaks of the importance of the "apostolic" formation of the children, their formation as men and women for others, whose horizons of concern extend beyond the limits of themselves and their own immediate families. The bishops discuss the role of the state in providing the means for parents to fulfill their educational responsibilities. When all is said and done, though, the parents themselves have the primary respon-sibility. Perhaps we could conclude this section by noting that this duty and privilege, while all-important, is tempo-rary. What I mean is that the children are entrusted to their parents for a time, usually for about 20 years. They do not own their children, nor can they make the children the ultimate center of their lives. They nurture and edu-cate them precisely to set them free, to enable them to move out into the world confident and unafraid. At that time the couple realize even more deeply the meaning of their own commitment to each other. They have commit-ted themselves, we might say, to save their souls together. For this reason the evening years of a good marriage can be the best of all. Having fought the good fight, the spouses can now dedicate themselves wholeheartedly and without reserve to the other end of marriage: the fostering

of mutual love. All that remains is eternal life and the
vision of the God who made them one.

The Mystery of the Single Life

Vatican II, and Christian spirituality in general, has
much to say about both marriage and the celibate religious
life. There is, however, a third way which receives very
little discussion: the single lay life in the world. If we
except references to what are called "secular institutes"
today I find only one mention of the single life in Vatican
II. It appears in chapter V of *Lumen Gentium*, the council's
fundamental constitution on the church. There the bishops apply the "universal call to holiness" to the various
members of the church. After discussing bishops, priests
and clerics, married couples and parents, we find the only
conciliar reference to the single life: "A like example, but
one given in a different way, is that offered by widows
and single people, who are able to make great contributions toward holiness and apostolic endeavor in the
Church" (No. 41).

What is that "different way" in which single women
and men provide an example, a sign or symbol, of
Christ's love for his bride, the church? The council does
not tell us. Nor do we find much reference to the single
life in church tradition. It is true that Paul, especially in 1
Corinthians 7, has high praise for those in the church
who remain unmarried. But once religious life was established, these passages were and are generally applied to
those vowed to celibacy. We could justly say that single
lay Christians are the forgotten people of Christian spirituality. I know that several of my single directees have
expressed their feeling of neglect. In the hope that this
lacuna will be filled in the years to come, I would like to
share a few personal reflections on the topic.

The first thing we must stress is that the universal
call to holiness applies to every member of the church.
What we have said about the laying of a solid spiritual

foundation applies to the single person as much as to anyone else. Moreover, as the council tells us, this call to holiness is precisely a call to embody in their own lives the love of Christ for his Father and for his church. Spouses do this by their love for one another, a love made fruitful (as is the love of Christ for his church) in their children. Celibate religious do it by the eschatological sign they live, that God can be our enough, and that in the end he will be "all in all" for every one of us. The problem with the single life is that it seems to overlap the other two Christian states of life. Like the celibate life it is eschatological, since the single person has no centering human love comparable to the spouse in marriage. But like the married life, being single is incarnational inasmuch as the single person is a member of the laity, called to live in the world and to transform the secular order from within.

Perhaps this problem, this ambivalence, can also be seen as the key to the real meaning and value of the single lay vocation. It occurs to me that the single lay person is uniquely qualified to serve as the bridge between the incarnational and the eschatological, between the church's meaningful presence to all our contemporary human concerns and her proclamation that the goal of all our striving is beyond the present, is eternal life with the Lord. If so, then the single lay life is indeed a challenging and difficult vocation. It is not easy to be a "bridge" between two worlds, as I said long ago in reflecting on the missionary's stance between two cultures (*Opening to God*, pp. 12-13). Bridges tend to get trampled on; they link two shores precisely by living in tension. It is the well-moderated tension which keeps a bridge in place and prevents it from collapsing. But it has to be well-constructed and secure in its foundations if it is to function well.

Concretely this means that the single person who is

solidly rooted in Christ can interpret the lay world to
celibates, and the celibate world to the married. They
partake of both without being fully identified with either.
Thus the single person can be a witness to the world that
celibacy is not an escapist irrelevance—that the celibate
can be truly involved in the human concerns of men and
women today. And she or he can witness to those living
the celibate life that a truly God-centered life is also
possible "in the world."

Like every vocation, this is not an easy one. The
single person can easily become a professional "old
maid"—concerned only about her own small, nicely
ordered, self-centered world. She—or he—can enjoy the
freedom to think only of her own needs and desires. Or,
if singleness was not chosen but just happened, she can
become embittered that life has passed her by. In either
case, she is too self-centered and has not learned that
happiness is found only by those who do not seek it too
anxiously or hoard it too greedily. But if her faith is real
and deep, the single person can find her state of life rich
in opportunities to love and to serve. She can be involved
in social service and parochial activities to a degree which
would not be possible for her married sister with a young
family. And, as her sister grows older and is widowed,
she can be a sign of hope to her, a sign that death, while
it is the end of marriage, is not the end of the world.

I have known women—and men—like that. There is
no doubt that their life is not easy. They must have come
to the state of blessed singleness only after many tears in
the lonely night. But, in one way or another, that is true
of every vocation. Marriage is "for better or worse," and
the worse is inevitable and essential to the whole mystery.
Similarly, life in a celibate community is not always a bed
of roses either. The married person has at least chosen her
own "poison"; the celibate religious lives with people he
or she has not chosen, with whom he or she may have

little natural compatibility. Despite the difficulties, however, there are happy celibates and fulfilled married people. By the grace of God there are happy, fulfilled single lay persons too. I have known some of them, and I thank the Lord for the gift of their lives.

All This Is Spirituality

In the Introduction to this book we raised the question whether there is any such thing as a specifically *lay* spirituality. It is a question I am often asked: Is there anything unique or distinctive about the spirituality of a lay person, or is it precisely the same as the spirituality of any committed Christian, priest or religious or lay? I said in the introduction that there is only one Christian spirituality, in the sense that all of us are called to live fully the gospel teaching of Jesus. He did not make any distinctions of persons or states of life in his call to take up our cross daily and follow him. There are, however, different ways of living the Jesus-life of the gospel. While each of us is called to live the whole gospel, because of our human finitude none of us can live it wholly. That is, none of us can capture the whole, infinite mystery of Jesus' love for the Father in one finite life. In this sense, then, there are different spiritualities, and lay spirituality *is* distinct and special.

This uniqueness should be much clearer to us after all we have seen in the present chapter. While our prayer life is the heart of our spirituality, the latter term includes much more than just our times of formal prayer. Work, family and marital relationships, recreation and sickness— all of our life is "spirituality." What we have been discussing in this chapter, for example about family planning and the single lay life, is not merely theology or morality. It is really spirituality. That is, it becomes part of the whole way of life which is our response to the loving initiative of God revealed in Christ Jesus. "We know that by turning everything to their good God cooperates with all those who love him, with all those whom he has called according to his purpose" (Rom 8:28).

I mentioned in Chapter VI that Rosemary Haughton's article, "Marriage and Virginity: Two Ways to One End," has been very helpful in my work with the seminarians at San Jose. They have to see their celibate vocation in the light of, and as complementary to, the vocation of marriage. Perhaps she can also help us here to appreciate more deeply the distinctive, authentic spirituality of the married life. Basic to her whole argument is the conviction that all Christian life is *developmental*. We are "on the way," becoming, growing—our life in Christ is not static and fixed and frozen. We cannot see Christian life as a mere defensive "holding the fort," preserving the faith against external enemies. As Rosemary Haughton says:

> There is one call, addressed to all Christians, married or single, and it is a call to leave all things and follow Christ. Perhaps the operative word of this command is "follow," which implies covering a distance. The apparently total separation between marriage and celibacy as Christian ways of living has been due, possibly, to the fact that we didn't sufficiently realize the Christian life as a development. St. Paul recognized it, calling some "still babes in Christ" and not yet "spiritual men"; but both were Christians.

Haughton does not intend to imply that celibates are the "mature" while married persons are merely "babes in Christ." But she does argue that family life and marriage provide the ideal climate for the process of Christian maturity or development. Both ways, celibacy and marriage, are good ways for committed Christians to come to maturity.

> Both begin as babes in Christ, and follow Christ patiently towards maturity. And it is interesting that the nearer to Christ any Christian comes, the less is there any important difference in the nature of his

"spirituality," as between married and celibate. . . .
This realization does not destroy or devalue the
difference in vocation, but it does indicate that the
difference is a temporary one, and—although
essential—one which we should, in a sense, be striving
to make obsolete.

This is why she says, in the title of the chapter, that
marriage and virginity are "two ways to one end." And,
later in the chapter she speaks of the progressive "virgini-
zation" of marriage, and of the way celibacy becomes
progressively more fruitful as celibates learn to reach out
to others in love.

Although the two vocations do converge in the end
(in heaven), they are two very different ways. To speak
specifically of marriage, it provides "good conditions for
the early growth of the 'babes in Christ.' " When we are
still children, the family—as Vatican II has said—provides
the ideal climate for Christian growth. Parents have the
primary responsibility for the education of their children—
precisely because education involves a total personal
formation, a maturing not merely of the mind but of the
whole human being. And normally this can only be
accomplished in the loving environment of the family. In
having and raising children (procreation *and* education),
parents live their own spirituality. The values they impart
are those they themselves hold to. And in being imparted
to others, these values become more real and deeply held
by the parents themselves. I have discovered, as have
many others, that I *learn* much more in teaching others
than I ever did in all my years as a student.

Not only the children, though, grow to maturity in a
good family environment. For the spouses themselves
their marriage is a "seminary," a seed bed for maturing.
Even if the husband and wife have both come from good,
loving families, it is still true, as Rosemary Haughton
says, that

no home is ideal; therefore the foundation of security (which each of them has received in their own childhood) is never completely secure; the assurance of love never absolutely sure. There is always a remaining fear, a continuing insecurity, even in the best possible conditions. And in most cases this insecurity is still very considerable, so that the young adult (even the much older adult) still requires a great deal of assurance of being loved, the support of a secure background, if he is to grow spiritually.

As in all maturing processes, of course, discipline and self-sacrifice are as essential as supportive, reassuring love. In a good marriage each partner has to help the other to grow. I must give as much as I receive. Our relationship must be (in the terminology of Thomas Harris in *I'm OK, You're OK*) adult-adult and not merely parent-child. At times I may be a parent to the child in you; you, too, will have to parent the child in me. But the give-and-take demanded by this reciprocal relationship should bring us to an adult-adult encounter in which we can not only support one another but face the world together in strength and confidence. It is here that Rosemary Haughton sees the celibate vocation as a sign to married people: a sign that it is possible for love to take us out of ourselves. "All I longed for long ago was you," as the old love song says—yes, but as I mature I love you *not merely* because you fulfill me. I love you now for your own sake, because you are you. Your happiness is my fulfillment. When I realize this, I have come to discover the real meaning of love. I have become mature.

In so doing, I have come—perhaps without realizing it—to the very heart of Christian spirituality. One who has learned to love a man or a woman in this way has fulfilled Jesus' own description of perfect discipleship: "I give you a new commandment: love one another; just as I have loved you, so you too must love one another. By this love you have for one another, everyone will know that you are my disciples" (Jn 13:34-35). The point I wished to make in this section is that all that we have said about Vatican II's teaching on marriage and family life is truly *spirituality*. Family planning, procreation and education, the fostering of mutual love—these are not just principles of moral theology, textbook guidelines for confessional practice. No! They are the very concrete ways in which most lay Christians live their relationships not only to one another but to the God and Father of Jesus Christ. They are "spirituality" just as much as the times spent at Mass and in formal prayer, and are essentially related to these times of prayer.

For the mature person all of life is one integrated whole. It may take us a long time, and much struggle, to come to that maturity. But it is the goal which gives meaning to the long years of struggle. And on the journey—to take a final thought from Rosemary Haughton—both the married person and the celibate stand as "signs" to each other. The celibate, as we have seen, is a sign to the married of their need to grow beyond childhood.

> Christian married people are, necessarily, immersed in the secular and the contingent. That is where God calls them to be, for the salvation of the world. But if they are content to be there, if they do not feel the pull of eternal life, they will be no use as witnesses, they will indeed have succumbed to the world. . . . The remedy for worldliness, however, is not the preservation of an outdated form of family and devotional life as a defense against the world. Rather it is an awareness that to be a Christian means to be always reaching beyond this world, while loving it and serving it.

This "reaching beyond this world" is what the celibate life "signs" to the married Christian. But there is a reciprocal sign function here too. That is, the married person also serves as a sign to the celibate—a sign that the "security and privilege" of religious life are only a nursery, a hothouse in which the religious can mature into a more complete self-giving. Perhaps Rosemary Haughton, as a married theologian, is uniquely situated to recognize and enunciate the sign value for celibates of married life. At least I have never heard from my fellow religious the vision she presents:

> Marriage is explicitly a way of life dedicated to loving other people. It is the need to love that makes family life a challenge as well as a framework of security. The giving of love both creates the environment which the immature Christian needs, and also offers, in itself, the challenge to maturity. Being loved makes people comfortable and happy and able to grow, but it also makes them want to love in return—not just the one who loves, but others in need of love.

We have travelled far in the spirit of Vatican II. Marriage is no longer merely a means to procreate children and, secondarily, to provide a remedy for human concupiscence. Nor is celibacy merely a renunciation of this secular, inferior world of flesh and blood. Both are authentic and integral ways of living the gospel and becoming fully human. Each, that is, is a genuine spirituality if it is lived in a truly Christian way. And in the last analysis, both ways lead to the one end: maturity in Christ Jesus.

♣ Chapter Eight

Seasons and Communities in Lay Spirituality

The Concentric Circles of Our Lives

One striking discovery which I have made in reflecting upon, and writing about, lay spirituality is the vastness of the topic. There is so much we could say that it is necessary, in a book of moderate length like this one, to select the most important themes—those which would be of greatest help to the committed lay Christian in realizing her or his desire to come closer to Jesus Christ in his church. The topic is one which should command much interest in the years to come. Please God, each author who tackles it will be able to enrich our understanding of the full meaning of the age of the laity into which the church has entered after Vatican II. In my own prayerful reflection it seemed to me that my job, in the present book, was to show that the church has indeed entered a new age, that Vatican II does represent a real turning point in the church's understanding of the gospel call of Jesus. In Part I we tried to gain a solid appreciation of both the newness and the historical continuity of Vatican II's vision of the church as the people of God.

The fruit for the reader of Part I, I would hope, is a deeper appreciation of both the reality and the realism of Jesus' call to holiness in the lay life. In his "good news" there are no class distinctions: The least is the greatest, and anyone who wishes to enter the kingdom of heaven must become like a little child. I suppose I have always known this is some vague way, but my reflection on and writing of Part I has certainly deepened my own appreciation of the radical, revolutionary beauty of Jesus' kingdom. The seating arrangement in heaven will surely be very different from ours here on earth. Many of the people who occupy the front seats in the orchestra (or the places of honor in church) here on earth may be fortunate to find standing room in the balcony at the heavenly festival. And they may be astounded to find the orchestra seats closest to the Lord's throne occupied by people whom they considered not worth noticing here on earth. Jesus' story of Dives and Lazarus (Lk 16:19-31) will prove to be all too painfully true.

We have to be careful, though, of a dangerous kind of reverse snobbery here. While it is true that the kingdom of heaven is for the poor and the pure of heart, the poverty and purity of which Jesus speaks is not easily achieved by anyone. He also tells us that discipleship is costly and demanding, that we must take up our cross daily to follow him. In a mysterious and challenging passage in Matthew's gospel, Jesus even says: "Since John the Baptist came, up to this present time, the kingdom of heaven has been subjected to violence and the violent are taking it by storm" (Mt 11:12). Whatever the precise meaning of Jesus' words (a question still debated by scripture scholars), it seems clear that we cannot claim heaven just because we happen to be materially poor—or because, like the Pharisee in Jesus' parable (Lk 18:9-14), we are not "grasping, unjust, adulterous like the rest of mankind." Christian holiness is not merely negative—we cannot claim eternal life merely because we are *not* rich, or not adulterous.

Thus it was that we sought in Part II to discover what we must do and be in order to claim the promised inheritance of the Lord. In Chapter V we discussed an interior program of spirituality suited to the lay life. And in

Chapters VI and VII we spoke of the necessary overflow of our inner life into the marketplace. Spirituality, we said, involves both prayer and action. Indeed, every aspect of our lives—including sexuality, raising a family, and earning a living—is a part of a Christian lay spirituality. This is why Vatican II can speak of a "universal call to holiness" which makes the lay person a priest, prophet and king in his or her vocation to transform, to "Christify" the secular world.

How often today I hear people complain that society is not what it used to be. The divorce rate is soaring, or, in countries like the Philippines where divorce is not allowed, more and more marriages are breaking up anyway. Sexual morality is increasingly lax. The drug problem has become a worldwide epidemic. Religious vocations are declining, at least in the industrialized world. And everywhere we live under the threatening cloud of nuclear warfare. It seems to many that we live in the worst of times. But is this the whole picture? I think not. Since antiquity, men and women (especially as they themselves grow older) have longed for the good old days when life was much better. The Roman poet spoke of the *laudator temporis acti*, and Eugene O'Neill built a famous play, *The Great God Brown*, on the universal illusion that things were better when we were young. This is not to claim, however, that things are better today. In my judgment this claim is just as unrealistic as its pessimistic opposite. Every age has its own sins and its own strengths. The real point is that this is the only age in which you and I are called to live. It is the only one on which we can hope to exert any influence for good. Lamenting the good old days can be a way of escaping our responsibility for the present.

It is indeed better to light one candle than to curse the darkness. But the fact remains that we are *social* beings. The church is a community of believers and, as

Three more times in this same paragraph, in discussing the transfer of priests and the establishment of parishes, the same criterion, "the good (or care) of souls," is repeated. Moreover, these phrases are found repeatedly in the preceding paragraph, which gives a profile of the ideal parish priest. His role involves "teaching, sanctifying and governing," all ordered to the good and growth of the members of his parish community. He should know them personally and should adapt his ministry to their concrete needs. He is neither a dictator nor a mere mechanical dispenser of the sacraments.

In the council's vision, the heart of the priest's ministry is the liturgical life of the parish.

> In discharging their duty to sanctify their people, pastors should arrange for the celebration of the Eucharistic Sacrifice to be the center and culmination of the whole life of the Christian community. They should labor to see that the faithful are nourished with spiritual food through the devout and frequent reception of the sacraments and through active and intelligent participation in the liturgy (No. 31).

The council also stresses the sacrament of penance, sound moral teaching, the inculcation of a genuine missionary and sharing spirit—but the heart and soul of all parochial life is the Holy Eucharist. As the bishops had said in the council's first decree, *On the Sacred Liturgy,* Jesus Christ

> is always present in His Church, especially in her liturgical celebrations. He is present in the sacrifice of the Mass, not only in the person of His minister. . . but especially under the Eucharistic species. . . . Rightly, then, the liturgy is considered as an exercise of the priestly office of Jesus Christ. . . . From this it follows that every liturgical celebration, because it is an action of Christ the priest and of His Body the Church, is a sacred action surpassing all others (No. 7).

A family or a people realizes its deepest unity in celebrating together. Without festive memories a people has no heart and no soul. And the same is true of the Christian community. What makes us one is that we *remember* the Lord with joy, we remember his passion and death and resurrection. "Do this in memory of me." That is, whenever you do this, whenever you celebrate the Eucharist, please remember me. Our Mass is not merely a duty or a ritual obligation—it is a joyous remembrance of the Lord's love for us unto death. "All I ask of you is forever to remember me as loving you." Because that memory and that love are at the very heart of our lives today, we are called together as a community every week. All the joys and sorrows, failures and successes, of the week are brought before the Lord. Since he has loved us unto death, we can be confident that nothing which happens to us today can ever be outside his concern or beyond the reach of his power.

The priest's primary responsibility, in the vision of Vatican II, is to make this confident assurance come alive for his people in the Holy Eucharist. The other works of the parish—counselling, social action, youth work, catechetics, prayer groups—are indeed important. But they are like the body of which the Eucharist is the soul. This is why the church has made Sunday Mass obligatory for Catholics. The body without the soul is lifeless. We need to come together *as one people* if we are to be truly alive in Christ. Sunday has been chosen for this communal celebration because it is the day of the Lord's resurrection. In the Old Testament the Sabbath day was Saturday. But for Christians, almost from the time of the apostles, Sunday has become the new Sabbath because Jesus' resurrection on Easter Sunday is the center of our faith and the bedrock of our hope. The important thing, however, is that our Sunday Eucharist is an act of *community* worship, and the community cannot gather in unity unless there is a set time for their gathering. How long would a family survive as one if everyone came to dinner whenever he or she wished?

The crucial point here is our realization that the Sunday Eucharist is the act of a worshipping community. If we see the Mass merely as a private act of worship, as an encounter between me and God (the way Catholics have often viewed it in the past), then the crowd at Sunday Mass will be little more than a bother and a distraction. Because this attitude did permeate much of our religious thinking in the recent past, the council devoted considerable energy and attention to the renewal of the liturgy. The Mass has been translated into the language of the people, and is now celebrated facing the congregation. Much stress is now placed on congregational responses, community singing and lay participation. The people are encouraged to receive communion frequently, if possible every time they attend Mass. And all of these changes, which seemed so revolutionary only 20 years ago, have as their primary purpose to make the Eucharist a truly living community celebration of the Lord's love.

Seasons of Grace

In many parishes, the liturgical changes called for by Vatican II have been beautifully implemented. Where this has been the case, the parish community has become a true extended family—alive, united and mutually supportive in facing the challenges of Christian life today. The unity realized and celebrated in the Mass naturally flows over into the other areas of parish life. And yet unfortunately, as we all know, the revitalization of parish life after Vatican II has proceeded unevenly. People often complain to me that their own parish is "dead." There is no parish life apart from the Mass and the celebration of the sacraments. And even this liturgical life is often cold and perfunctory, more like a crowd in a supermarket than a family celebrating together. In most parishes the situation is not so bleak—but neither does it measure up to the ideal proposed by Vatican II. Why is this so? As we have seen, the council makes the parish priest primarily responsible for the vitality of his parish. Many priests, however, were themselves formed in an earlier, pre-Vatican II age so they find it difficult to enter into the communal spirit of the new liturgy. They cannot give to others what they do not possess themselves.

What can we do to improve the situation? I would like to make just two points in this section. First, the primary problem is one of proper instruction and explanation. I recall the Sunday, some 20 years ago, when the new liturgy was first introduced. I was recently ordained and was assisting an older priest in his parish. The American bishops had just introduced congregational singing into the liturgy, and this priest was a loyal and obedient son of the hierarchy. So he began the Mass by announcing that the church had commanded all Catholics to sing at Mass. No matter that the congregation had been silent and passive for generations: If the pope wanted us to sing, sing we would! The result was predictable: The organist played and practically no one sang. For the priest this was an act of defiance. He stopped the music, and proclaimed with restrained anger, "The church has commanded us to sing. If you do not wish to obey, then please leave the church." As far as I know, no one left the church. But very few sang either. The people were not prepared for the sudden change in their lifelong habits. They were not defiant, but they were confused and ill at ease. They had not been properly prepared for the change, nor did they understand why they were suddenly being asked to participate more actively in the Mass. Like a dear aunt of mine, they were accustomed to the old way, where the priest said his Mass and she said her rosary and each avoided distracting the other.

This brings us to the second point I would like to make. Most of us have become comfortable with the congregational participation which seemed so strange only 20 years ago. Very few would really like to go back to the days when the Mass was celebrated in a strange language by a priest facing the wall. But these changes, revolutionary as they may have seemed and important as they are in making the Eucharist a truly communal act of worship, are not the whole story. The church has revised the whole *structure* of the eucharistic celebration, and in so doing has sought to recapture what it meant to the early church. The first generation of Christians still thought of themselves as Jews—reformed Jews, we might say. They continued to go "as a body to the Temple every day but met in their houses for the breaking of bread" (Acts 2:46; see 5:12). Apparently their synagogue service was supplemented at home by the "breaking of bread," their celebration of the Lord's supper in response to his command to "do this as a memorial of me" (Lk 22:19). Only as persecution drove them out of the Jewish community did they transfer the synagogue service to their homes.

We have here the origin of the two parts of our Mass: the liturgy of the word or scripture (the old synagogue service at which Jesus preached in beginning his public ministry in Luke 4:16-22) and the liturgy of the breaking of the bread, which begins with the offertory. In the old days one could fulfill his or her Sunday Mass obligation by arriving in time for the offertory. We now realize, however, that the liturgy of the word is just as central to our faith as the liturgy of consecration and communion. As the fathers of the church used to say, we are fed at two tables: the table of the word of God and the table of Holy Communion. In recapturing their vision we Catholics are rediscovering what our Protestant brethren have always stressed: the importance of the Bible to our faith, not

merely as a source of church dogma but as a living guide
for the daily life of every Christian.

The changes in the second part of the Mass, such as
the introduction of several eucharistic prayers and communion in the hand, are probably well understood and
well accepted by most committed Catholics today. In the
liturgy of the word, though, we still need more instruction and explanation. Pope Paul VI, following the mandate
of Vatican II, introduced a whole new cycle of scripture
readings for the first part of the Mass. It is designed so
that every Catholic who attends Sunday Mass regularly
will hear virtually the whole of the gospels every three
years.[1]

The first reading from the Old Testament is chosen to
reflect the central theme of the gospel reading; and the
second reading, generally from the New Testament epistles, can also be related to the gospel. Thus the gospel
reading sets the theme for every Sunday Eucharist. This it
is that gives the whole Mass a beautiful and relevant
unity. In preparing my Sunday homily, I always look first
at the gospel to discover the theme of the liturgy. But then
it is important to compare the gospel with the first two
readings. In this way we can discover which aspect of
Jesus' teaching the church desires to emphasize in this
Mass.

The lay person can also prepare to enter more deeply
into the liturgy by prayerfully reading over the Mass texts
for the following Sunday. Many parishes list the daily
scripture readings in their weekly bulletins. And there are
several good inexpensive missals available, the best

---

[1] The daily liturgy has also been extensively revised, so that daily
Mass-goers will hear the gospels every year and a representative
sampling of the epistles and Old Testament writings every two years.
Here, too, the church highly recommends a brief daily homily—to
reveal the treasures of the Bible and to apply them to the daily lives of
those in the congregation.

known in the United States and the Philippines being the St. Joseph Missal and the Vatican II Missal of the Daughters of St. Paul. Moreover, Pope Paul VI insisted that the priest should normally preach a *homily* and not a sermon. That is, he should explain the scripture readings and apply them to the lives of his people. While sermons, which are topical discussions of such matters as birth control, social justice and the obligation to vote, are occasionally necessary, they should be the exception rather than the rule. The primary purpose of the homily is to open up to the people the treasures of the biblical word of God. In this way we are fed at the table of the word—the first of the two tables on which the eucharistic banquet is served.

The church's year is divided into what is known as the "ordinary time" and the special seasons, like Advent and Christmas, Lent, Easter and Pentecost. These special seasons of grace have their own liturgy commemorating the great events of our redemption. Thus the church's New Year's Day is not January 1st but rather the first Sunday of Advent. Advent is the beautiful season of longing and expectation and hope. It culminates in the celebration of Christmas, in which all three comings of Jesus—in Bethlehem, in our hearts today, and as Lord of Glory at the end of time—are joyously proclaimed. The "ordinary time" of the year commences after the Feast of the Epiphany and continues, with an interruption for Lent and the Easter season, for 34 Sundays until the end of November. The ordinary time is a quiet time in the liturgy. But it is not merely a period of waiting for the next festive season. During the ordinary time we journey with the Lord in his public ministry. Like the first disciples, we observe him and listen to his teaching. We discover in depth and in detail what it means to live our lives with him—and we begin to see the gospel meaning of our own ordinary daily lives.

The most important of all the liturgical seasons of grace is Holy Week and Easter. The heart of our faith is the paschal mystery of the passion, resurrection and ascension of our Lord, for which the first several weeks of Lent prepare us by calling us to conversion. The primary themes of these weeks are prayer, penance and good works. And then, as we move into the final weeks of Lent, the focus of the liturgy shifts to the final days and weeks of Jesus' own life. Thus it is that Holy Week itself is not really a time of sorrow for sin and repentance, our proper concern in the early weeks of Lent, but rather of gratitude to the Lord that he has loved us, despite our unworthiness, even unto death. Then, on Easter Sunday and in the weeks that follow, we proclaim our faith that the Lord has not only died for us but has conquered death. With St. Paul we cry exultantly to all the world that

> if Christ has not been raised you are still in your sins. And what is more serious, all who have died in Christ have perished. If our hope in Christ has been for this life only, we are the most unfortunate of all people. But Christ has in fact been raised from the dead, the first fruits of all who have fallen asleep (1 Cor 15:17-20).

Prayer Communities and Apostolic Associations

The eucharistic liturgy, with its annual cycle of seasons of grace, provides the framework for and sets the tone of our Christian life. As we have stressed throughout this book, however, we come before God as a community, as his people. The central expression of our identity as a believing community is our gathering together, in the extended family of the parish, to celebrate the Eucharist, especially on Sunday. In the church's tradition, every Sunday is a celebration of the paschal mystery: Every Sunday is, in a sense, Easter Sunday. But in order that the liturgy come alive for us, it must overflow into our

daily lives. We must prepare for it, for example by reading
over in advance the scripture passages for the coming
Sunday Mass. And we must take seriously the final
words of the celebrant, "The Mass is ended. Let us go in
peace, to love and serve the Lord."

Both our preparation for and our living out of the
Mass are, or can be, communal activities. In the Philippines today many small communities have weekly prayer
meetings in which the scripture readings for the coming
Sundays are read, discussed and prayed over. Some are
barrio gatherings, guided by our seminarians or by sisters
or committed lay leaders. There are also many charismatic
prayer communities whose prayer life together is centered
on the scripture and the liturgy. I know of, and work
with, such groups composed of workers in the same
office or of men and women in the same professions. On
the whole these movements are one of the most encour-
aging signs of the vitality of the church's faith life today.
Not only are people praying but they are praying *as a
community*.

The church after Vatican II has frequently blessed
and encouraged these prayer communities, which first
emerged in the late 1960s shortly after the council ended.
But she has also warned us of certain dangers. A prayer
group should not replace or compete with the liturgical
worship of the parish community. It should not foster an
elitist mentality which tends to look down upon non-
members as less Catholic or less holy. It should have
sound guidance, especially in understanding scripture
and the real nature of Christian prayer. The best and
healthiest groups I know of do seek such guidance. And
truly committed priests and religious will be prepared to
provide whatever help they can, both by explaining prayer
and the scripture and by helping the community to
discern the good from the evil spirit in their midst. As we
noted in speaking of St. Francis de Sales, the devil will

always be working to corrupt our good desires and good works. This is not a sign that something is wrong with us. Quite the opposite! The closer we come to God and the more we seek to grow, the more active the devil will be in seeking to derail us.[2]

One sure sign that a prayer community is on the right track is the presence of the fruits of the Spirit in their life together: love, joy, peace, patience, kindness, goodness, trustfulness, gentleness and self-control (Gal 5:22). Another good and reliable sign is their attitude toward those who are not members of the community. Their life in Christ should make them more loving and more tolerant of others. There should be no attempt to make everyone else dance to *their* music. And the community should not be a ghetto, inbred and narrow and pharisaical. There are many ways to God. He takes each of us in our own uniqueness and reaches out to us where we are. Those of us who are truly his children owe it to him to be as open and accepting of others as he is.

While a prayer community (or an individual pray-er) should not try to dragoon others into their form of spirituality, there should be a real apostolic thrust to their lives. That is, the community's prayer life should overflow in service to the wider world around them. Vatican II was so convinced of this that the bishops devoted an entire document to *The Apostolate of the Laity*. They say that this apostolate can be engaged in "either as individuals or as members of groups or associations" (No. 15). Much will depend on the circumstances of each person's life, as well as on her or his own temperament and sense of personal call. What is important in every case is that "the laity should vivify their lives with charity and express it as best

---

[2] I discussed the importance of discernment in *Weeds Among the Wheat* (Ave Maria Press, 1984). Chapter 7, on the discernment of consolation, would be especially relevant in guiding a charismatic community.

they can in their works" (No. 16). While valuing highly
the works of charity performed by individuals, the council
also reflects its essentially ecclesial, communitarian thrust
when it says:

> They should remember, nevertheless, that human
> beings are naturally social, and that it has pleased God
> to unite those who believe in Christ in the People of
> God (cf. 1 Peter 2:5-10) and into one body (cf. 1
> Corinthians 12:12). Hence the group apostolate of
> Christian believers happily corresponds to a human
> and Christian need and at the same time signifies the
> communion and unity of the Church in Christ (No.
> 18).

Apostolic associations have several values, for the
person and for the apostolate itself; they "sustain their
members, form them for the apostolate, and rightly
organize and regulate their apostolic work so that much
better results can be expected than if each member were
to act on his own" (No. 18).

The council avoided a detailed discussion of particular apostolic organizations, wishing instead to stress the
basic principles which should always be normative: union
with the church, responsiveness to the needs of time and
place, sound and effective organization, and that genuine
charity which embodies and reveals to all people the love
of Christ for the world. It stresses the value of various
associations formed to pursue "catholic action" in the
factories, among the farmers and in almost every social
milieu—especially in situations of poverty, neglect and
oppression.

Such associations, while they must be based on
sound Christian doctrine and moral principles, are again
the proper apostolate of the laity. The council reminds us
that just as prayer communities should not be inbred and
self-centered, so too apostolic organizations should never
lose the prayerful spirit which gives life and meaning to

all their works. To ensure coordination Vatican II recommends that councils of the laity be established on the diocesan and national levels, and that a "special secretariat . . . be established at the Holy See (in Rome) for the service and encouragement of the lay apostolate" (No. 26). It also devotes the whole of chapter 6 of *The Apostolate of the Laity* to a discussion of the crucial question of proper formation for the lay apostolate.

The ideal, then, is a blend or union of the interior and the exterior, of the chapel and the marketplace. In this way we can be sure, as I explained in *Darkness in the Marketplace* (chapter III), that we are "doing God's work" and not merely "working for God." That is, we want to be doing what *he* wants us to do, and not merely what we think he should want. Many organizations, like many individuals, work very hard to meet the problems which they perceive as urgent. But the world is vast, and the needs of people are virtually infinite. The challenge is to discern what the Lord desires *us* (or me) to do in the building up of his kingdom on earth. None of us is called to meet every need.

All that we have said in the preceding paragraph would apply equally well to religious congregations and secular institutes in the church. Thus it is good to recall from Chapter IV that the specific mission of the laity is to sanctify the secular world *from within*—to be the leaven in the dough of the world. The council fathers explore the specific ways in which the laity can exercise this more direct form of apostolate. For example, they stress the value of the laity who "in extremely trying circumstances do what they can to take the place of priests" (No.17) by teaching Christian doctrine, forming prayer communities, etc. In the Mindanao church of the Southern Philippines, a frontier area where priests and religious have been relatively scarce until recently, the lay ministry (*kaabag*) program has been a notable example of this direct lay

apostolate in isolated areas and even in situations of
persecution.

While the council does value and encourage the
collaboration of the laity in the liturgical and sacramental
life of the church, the bishops also stress the apostolic role
which *only* lay women and men can fill. For example, a
good friend of mine realized, during his latest annual
retreat, that his apostolate had to extend to his place of
work—that he had a mission to the people he worked
with in the business world, a mission which no clergy-
man or sister could accomplish. At the time of his retreat,
it was not very clear to either of us what precisely this call
might entail, although it did seem to be the Lord's word
to him. He returned to his marketplace open to whatever
opportunities might arise. And the Lord quickly revealed
what precisely he had in mind, not only for my friend but
also for his equally committed wife. They discovered a
prophetic role for themselves which gave a new meaning
to their lay vocation and a richer relevance to their life of
prayer.

Open to the Wider World

We have seen in the preceding sections of this chapter that the lay person lives his or her Christian life at
many levels, in ever-widening circles. At the core is one's
personal relationship to the Lord. But this relationship is
lived within the family, the parish community, the work
environment and civil society. The council speaks of the
lay person's role in civil society in a beautiful paragraph of
the decree on *The Apostolate of the Laity*. It is found in
chapter III, on the various fields of the apostolate which
are proper to the laity:

> The apostolate of the social milieu, that is, the effort to
> infuse a Christian spirit into the mentality, customs,
> laws, and structures of the community in which a
> person lives, is so much the duty and responsibility of
> the laity that it can never be properly performed by

others. In this area the laity can exercise the apostolate of like toward like. It is here that lay people add to the testimony of life the testimony of their speech; it is here in the arena of their labor, profession, studies, residence, leisure and companionship that the laity have a special responsibility to help their brothers (No. 13).

The reference here is to the secular sphere which *Lumen Gentium* describes as the proper arena of the lay vocation. The council was also concerned, however, that the laity not be narrow or parochial in their concerns. One who follows Jesus Christ must have a heart as open to the whole world as his was. While we do have a special responsibility for the time and place in which we live, our horizons should not be nationalistic or chauvinistic. Thus, in the decree on the lay apostolate, the bishops of Vatican II insist that Christians

> should be concerned about the needs of the People of God dispersed throughout the world. They should above all make missionary activity their own by giving material or even personal assistance, for it is a duty and honor for Christians to return to God a part of the good things which they receive from Him (No. 10).

I am reminded of my own days in a parochial elementary school in Rochester in the 1940s. The sisters made us children aware in many ways of the needs of missionaries and of people in mission lands. Little did I then dream that I would one day be a missionary myself, but I am sure the seed of that vocation was sown by the nuns during my earliest years.

Not everyone, of course, is called to be a missionary as I was. But I would hope that the same spirit touched and changed the lives even of my classmates who were to live their whole lives in Rochester. It is really to them that the council is speaking. Similarly, when the bishops speak of the importance of international apostolic organizations, they are not only addressing world travellers and those who live their lives on the global stage. Each of us, however humble our life may be, is a citizen of the world, especially in this age of global communication and international trade. When I was a boy, starvation in the Sudan was not as real to a child in America: By the time we had read about it, the starving people half-a-world away were already dead. Today we see and read about events as they are happening.

There is a danger here, of course. The information explosion can engender a sense of helplessness and hopelessness in the face of problems so vast and so distant. The temptation can be strong to imitate the smoker who, because he read in the newspaper that smoking causes cancer, stopped reading the newspapers! Or we can allow ourselves to be overwhelmed by problems over which we seem to have no control. Neither, however, is the Christian solution. The disciple of Jesus must have a heart large enough to embrace the whole world, but he or she must also have a strong sense of faith and trust. The world belongs to God, not to me. Ultimately all these problems are *his* concern, his responsibility. But because I love him I share his concern, in the sense that I wish to be his instrument in whatever way he wishes to work through me for the good of his people. And, above all, my prayer, like that of the Little Flower, is worldwide in its scope.

It is in this spirit that Vatican II, in *The Church in the Modern World*, speaks of the involvement of the laity in political life. Not all of us can aspire to high political office. But every one of us can vote, can take an interest in the important issues of our time and help to choose men and women who will speak to these issues in a truly human and Christian way. Here indeed is a concrete test of your grasp of the whole meaning of this book: If voting seems irrelevant to your life in Christ, then the real point of Vatican II and of this book has been missed. The secular and the sacred would still be worlds apart. And "the age of the laity" would be but an empty phrase.

The Goal of All Our Striving

In the final chapter of *When the Well Runs Dry*, the book in which I sought to describe and explain the mysterious experience of one who matures in prayer "beyond the beginnings," I quoted a favorite passage from T. S. Eliot's *Four Quartets*. In "Little Gidding, V" Eliot says,

> With the drawing of this Love
> And the voice of this calling
> We shall not cease from exploration.
> And the end of all our exploring
> Will be to arrive where we started
> And know the place for the first time.

I am reminded of these lines as we come to the end of our discussion of lay spirituality today. The areas we have discussed such as marriage and family life, work and politics, prayer and the sacraments are all part of the ordinary experience of any committed lay Christian. Even the new light cast on all of these areas by Vatican II's inauguration of the age of the laity is not really new in the sense that it is solidly rooted in the gospel teaching of Jesus himself. In a true sense we have managed "to arrive where we started."

And yet there is a real novelty here, the novelty of *discovering* what we have (or should have) always known. Long ago St. Benedict had to call us back to the gospel truth concerning holiness: that it is not extraordinary deeds that bring us close to God, but the extraordinary love with which we do and view the ordinary in our lives. For many of his disciples, Benedict's call to make the Sermon on the Mount the only rule of their lives must have seemed both ancient and new. Like most great discoveries in the sciences, it must have seemed obvious once Benedict proclaimed it. The exciting novelty was in really knowing for the first time the place we had always "known."

The essential message of Vatican II to the church today is much like Benedict's call to his monks over 1,500 years ago. Holiness is to be found in the most ordinary circumstances of our lives, although holiness itself is not at all ordinary. It takes extraordinary faith and trust and love to see the ordinary through the eyes of God. As Eliot says, "we shall not cease from exploration." Zacchaeus, in one sense, did not have to climb the tree in order to encounter Jesus. And yet, in another sense, perhaps he did. That is, he had to be willing to make a fool of himself in his search for the right way and the right place to encounter the Lord. Only then could Jesus call him back to the ground, to his daily life and experience—now with eyes opened and cleansed, so as to be able to see what was always there.

As we come to the end of our time of exploration together, my prayer is that you who are called to the lay life can see more deeply the richness and the beauty of your call. Surely this is not "the end of all our exploring." But maybe it can be the end of the beginning—as Zacchaeus' descent from the sycamore tree was for him.

♣ Epilogue

The Universal Call to Happiness

The Goal of Our Christian Life

Whenever we take a journey, it is important that we are clear on our goal, our destination. Only then can we know the best road to travel and the most suitable means of transportation. As we have seen throughout this book, the Christian life is a journey toward God and toward our own fullness of life as human beings and as his children. In Part I we traced the journey of the church through the past 2,000 years, and we saw her gradual discovery of the deeper meaning of the incarnation of her Lord and Savior, Jesus Christ. And in Part II we have also considered the life of the individual lay Christian and of the communities in which she or he lives, again as a journey, a process of growth.

It should be clear by now that the goal for every Christian is holiness, that is, to be made perfect as our heavenly Father is perfect. We know, however, that this goal is not completely realized in this life. And so, in chapter VII of *The Constitution on the Church*, the bishops of Vatican II invite us to consider the eternal, heavenly goal of our journey. While authentic Christianity is not an escapist pie-in-the-sky or opium of the masses (as I hope we have also made abundantly clear in this book), we do believe that we do not have here a lasting city. Important as this life and this world are to our Christian faith, they are not the end of the story. Chapter VII of *Lumen Gentium* expresses this conviction in its somewhat unwieldy title, "The Eschatological Nature of the Pilgrim Church and Her Union with the Heavenly Church."

The word *eschatological* refers to the end-time, the final reality of death, judgment and eternal life. The church has always been seen as a pilgrim, one on a religious journey. And the goal of her pilgrimage is eternal life, when she will be united forever and perfectly with Christ her Head. As the Second Vatican Council expresses it:

> The Church, to which we are called in Christ Jesus, and in which we will acquire sanctity through the grace of God, will attain her full perfection only in the glory of heaven. Then will come the time of the restoration of all things (Acts 3:21). Then the human race as well as the entire world, which is intimately related to man and achieves its purpose through him, will be perfectly re-established in Christ (No. 48).

This is our goal and our firm hope. It gives meaning to all of our efforts here and now to proclaim the gospel to all men and women. It is the reason for the lay person's vocation to transform and perfect the secular order. In the end none of our labors in this world will be wasted, provided only we see them in relation to the ultimate end of creation—and not as ends in themselves. Because, however, it is so easy for us to lose sight of our goal and to become swallowed up by the concerns of today as if they were an end in themselves, the council fathers cite numerous New Testament passages which affirm our confident hope for the future: e.g., Ephesians 1:10, Colossians 1:20, 2 Peter 3:10-13, John 12:32, Romans 8:19-22, 1 John 3:2. One has only to read these passages prayerfully in order to experience the hope which gives meaning to all of our day-by-day struggles, to truly believe that "the sufferings of the present time are not worthy to be compared with the glory to come that will be revealed in us" (Rom 8:18).

From the earliest days of the church, moreover, Christians have believed that our victory is not only in the future. Even now we are united in the "mystical body" of Christ with all those who have gone before us. This is the communion of saints, the union of the church militant (ourselves), the church suffering (the souls in purgatory) and the church triumphant (those already in heaven). Death does not break our unity or dissolve the church. And so we pray *for* those in purgatory, who have died in faith and belong to Christ but who still need to be transformed that they may fully possess the Lord. And we pray *to* the "saints" (not only those who are canonized but all who have won the final victory) that they will accompany us and encourage us who are still "on the way." Together with both we form one church. They are our extended family in faith, and we all give glory to God together, each in his or her own special way.

Properly understood, the communion of saints is a great source of joy and hope for us who are still pilgrims. As Vatican II says:

> Let the faithful be taught, therefore, that the authentic cult of the saints consists not so much in the multiplying of external acts, but rather in the intensity of our active love. . . . We seek from the saints' example in their way of life, fellowship in their communion, and aid by their intercession. At the same time, let the people be instructed that our communion with those in heaven, provided that it is understood in the more adequate light of faith, in no way weakens, but rather more thoroughly enriches the supreme worship we give to God the Father, through Christ, in the Spirit (No. 51).

Holiness and Happiness

In reflecting on the mystery of the communion of

saints, I am reminded of two suggestions which I received
while planning this book. I asked many friends what they
felt should be included in a discussion of lay spirituality.
A Jesuit friend in Australia wrote: "Listening over the last
quarter of a century to the inner confidences of Catholics
brought up in most parts of the world, I have the ever-
increasing impression that the well-known snake manages
quite successfully to keep us tied up in the kind of knots
that stifle growth. He or someone or something has
planted very cunningly in most of us the rumor that God
does not really love us. We can keep hearing the words, 'I
love you with an everlasting love,' and still live as though
we are not convinced that it is true." And a soon-to-be-
ordained seminarian in the Philippines wrote a note to the
same effect. He had been reflecting on the beautiful line
from Psalm 33: "Happy the nation whose God is the
Lord, the people whom He has chosen to be His own"(Ps
33:12). And he suggested I apply it to the liturgy: "Perhaps the theme of happiness manifested by means of
joyful celebrations could be developed—in contrast to the
usual serious and long-faced mood of our liturgical celebrations. I think this theme of happiness would suggest a
healthy change of mood for Filipino religious experience."

    The words of my friends have echoed in my mind
throughout the writing of these chapters, especially when
I was considering Vatican II's discussion of "the universal
call to holiness." To be holy is necessarily to be happy, at
least if we believe the witness of scripture. For example, it
is amazing how many psalms proclaim the happiness, the
blessedness of the people or the person whom the Lord
has chosen for his own.[1] And the New Testament is filled
with rejoicing by those who have been touched by the
Lord. To cite just one such passage, which may be my

---

[1]   Some of those which struck me especially are, besides Psalm 33:12,
the following: 21:2, 32:1, 47:1, 100, 146:5.

own favorite in the whole of scripture, John's First Epistle
begins with these beautiful words:

> Something which has existed since the begin-
> ning,
> that we have heard,
> and we have seen with our own eyes;
> that we have watched and touched with our
> hands;
> the Word, who is life—
> this is our subject.
> What we have seen and heard
> we are telling you
> so that you too may be in union with us,
> as we are in union
> with the Father
> and with His Son Jesus Christ.
> We are writing this to you to make our own joy
> complete (1 Jn 1:1,3-4).

John shares his experience of the Lord in order to
share his joy, and by sharing it with others, with us, to
come to the fullness of joy himself. He can only keep the
Lord he has found by giving him away. The happiness of
others completes his own happiness. It is striking that St.
Thomas Aquinas and the other great theologians of the
church have always appealed to this same principle in
explaining the creation of the world. Why did God make
us? Because, they say, *"bonum est diffusivum sui."* That is,
since God is all-good, his very nature demanded that he
share his goodness with others. He creates and redeems
out of a desire to share his happiness, his joy with us.
Thus to be godly or holy is to be good—and to be good is
to be happy.

This is why I have said so often in conferences to
religious and lay groups that a gloomy Christian is a
contradiction in terms. There are always, as we have seen
throughout this book, crises and challenges in the living

of our life of faith. To be happy does not necessarily mean to be carefree. But the true follower of Jesus is happy even in the midst of trials and bereavement, happy, we might say, deep in the heart even when there are storms on the surface. Happy because he or she is secure in the Lord's love, confident that he cares and that his power is equal to whatever life may bring.

To be realistic, though, we must admit that such happiness is the fruit of long experience of God's fidelity. In the last analysis, it is not what we read or what others tell us that leads us to trust him; it is, rather, our own experience of his loving care and fidelity in our own lives. The experience and the encouragement of others can lead us to take the risk of trusting the Lord—but real, secure happiness in him is the fruit of our own experience. The truly happy person is loving, mature, holy.

Mary, the Mother of the Church

It is most fitting that we conclude our discussion of lay spirituality with a word about the Blessed Virgin Mary. She was *the* truly happy disciple of her Son Jesus, as her *Magnificat* (Luke 1:46-55) proclaims so beautifully. Her soul glorified the Lord because of the great things he had done in her life. And she stands as the greatest inspiration to all of us who have not yet been able to say with full freedom: "I am the servant of the Lord: do with me as you have proposed." This is why the bishops in Vatican II chose to conclude their central *Constitution on the Church* with a discussion of the true and proper role of Mary in our Christian lives.

To understand the context of their desire that the Virgin Mary's role be properly understood, let us recall that in recent years there has been much concern about ecumenical prayer groups in the Philippines and else-where. The Second Vatican Council gave the initial impetus to what we call ecumenism today. And they praised it highly—provided only that it is properly understood.

Ecumenism is the name for dialogue among those from different faiths and even different Christian sects. It presupposes, as the council insists, that the participants come together solidly rooted in their own respective faiths. Ecumenism is not a means to attempt to convert others to my way of thinking, nor to attack their beliefs. It is a way for each participant to come to a deeper appreciation of her or his own faith. It is also an opportunity to be enriched by sharing the diverse perspectives and experiences of other sincere believers.

This is the ideal. In actual practice, however, many so-called ecumenical prayer groups have become the means to seek to challenge and shake the faith of the Catholic participants. And one of the main challenges is to the Catholic's devotion to the Blessed Virgin Mary. Don't we exaggerate her importance, even to the extent of making her equal to, or more important than, Jesus himself? And in so doing, are we not contradicting the scriptural revelation? The great problem is that most Catholics do not know how to answer these questions. Thus, if they cannot ask someone who does know, their faith may be shaken and even destroyed.

We can admit that popular piety, especially in a matriarchal society, may well exaggerate the role of Mary. There are always distortions in popular piety (for example, some cultures tend to be much more legalistic than Jesus was), but the church's *authentic* tradition concerning the role of the Blessed Virgin Mary is not guilty of the charges leveled above. Even before the current ecumenical movement became popular, Vatican II concluded its basic document on the church with a beautiful and balanced discussion of the place of Mary in the mystery of salvation.

The council deliberately included its consideration of the Blessed Virgin as the final section of *Lumen Gentium*, rather than in a separate document, in order to stress that

Mary is truly a member of the church, truly redeemed by Jesus Christ as we are, truly one of us. All of her graces and privileges (for which the Muslims also have great reverence) are because of the redemptive death and resurrection of her beloved Son. Moreover, as the council stresses, she lived by faith as we must. She and St. Joseph "did not understand the reply of their Son" when they found him in the temple. "But His Mother, to be sure, kept all these things to be pondered over in her heart (cf. Luke 2:41-51)" (No. 57).

It is because of her living faith that Mary is said to have cooperated in the redeeming work of her Son, Jesus. And in this she is a mother and model for us as we cooperate in the work of redemption today. "In an utterly singular way she cooperated by her obedience, faith, hope and burning charity in the Savior's work of restoring supernatural life to souls. For this reason she is a mother to us in the order of grace" (No. 61). Because she lived by faith and hope and love as we too must live, she can understand our life with its joys and trials. Because she lived *our* life perfectly, she can be a model and an inspiration to us.

There is one further truth about the life of the Blessed Virgin Mary which can form a fitting conclusion to our whole discussion of lay spirituality. She was a lay woman! In our contemporary categories, she, like St. Joseph, was not a nun or a cleric but a member of the laity. When you think of it, it is strange that Christians could ever have doubted that holiness was possible "in the world," considering that the two first disciples of Jesus, his mother and foster father, were called by God to a secular, lay life.

It is true, as we have seen throughout this book, that the committed lay life is difficult and challenging. But this is not because the world is evil and is hopelessly irreconcilable to God. Rather it is because real commitment to

Jesus, whether as a priest or as a sister or as a layperson, requires maturity and discernment. Vatican II has initiated the age of the laity by making clear to us all that lay women and men, like Mary and Joseph, are called to the fullness of Christian life and love. It is my prayer, as we conclude our reflections, that these chapters will be a source of inspiration and encouragement, and thus of happiness, to the many lay men and women who seek to follow the Lord in a truly challenging vocation.

Zacchaeus thought he had to climb a tree "because he was a little man and could not see Jesus because of the crowd" (Luke 19:3). But when Jesus came to that place, he looked up and said to Zacchaeus, 'Hurry down, Zacchaeus, because I must stay in your house today.' So Zacchaeus hurried down and welcomed him *with great joy.*" The beautiful lesson for us is this: Zacchaeus did not have to climb the tree of religious life to see the Lord. Jesus could encounter him right on the ground of his littleness—and could bring happiness to his own house by making it the resting place of God.